Praise for *What ar*

CU01023920

Richard Bustin has written an exceller
which matters most – what teachers shoula actually teach. He makes a
strong case for powerful knowledge, in both theory and practice, and
does something which is unfortunately rare: he looks at each school subject, or groups of subjects, and asks what knowledge matters most. A
terrific book.

**Professor Barnaby Lenon CBE, Dean, Faculty of Education,
University of Buckingham**

What are we Teaching? offers school leaders and teachers a profound
opportunity to reflect on the crucial role of subject specialist teachers
and their contributions to a subject-based curriculum. Drawing upon
research with educators across various subjects, the book captures the
authentic voices of teachers in art, design and technology, drama,
English, history, mathematics, modern foreign languages, music, physical education, religious education, and science. Alongside the teachers'
insights, explorations of knowledge within these subject areas illuminate
the potential for each subject to contribute distinctively to young people's education.

Dr Grace Healy, Education Director (Secondary), David Ross Education Trust

Richard Bustin's book is a much-needed addition to the academic discussion on the meaning and role of subjects in school education. Much has
previously been written about the concept of powerful knowledge and its
potential to highlight the importance of specialised knowledge in education: scholars in several discipline-based subject groups – for example, in
geography and history – have studied it, but most of this work has been
done in the context of these individual subjects. In this book, Richard
looks at different subjects and gives voice to teachers themselves. In the
theoretical part of the book, he makes a clear introduction to the concepts of powerful knowledge and the capability approach to help
teachers explore what kind of contribution their subjects can have for
their students. Even though the book is mainly targeted at readers in the
UK, it also works well for the international audience interested in the role
of subject-based education. I highly recommend this book to all teachers,
teacher educators and student teachers.

**Sirpa Tani, Professor of Geography and Environmental Education,
University of Helsinki, Finland**

This is a remarkable book and the timing of it is impeccable. The 2024 Labour Government is strongly committed to social justice and is looking to restore the *promise* of education. This book should inform that work. It is well informed, showing up some of the snake oil solutions of recent years, and through its conceptual framing provides a way to avoid the familiar swing of the educational pendulum. And Richard Bustin makes no bones about it: we need to trust teachers and support them properly in the 'knowledge work' which I fervently believe underpins great teaching at all levels.

It is not a 'practical' handbook, but it is written mainly for teachers and the voices of teachers are loud. The book advocates for the rich and enriching intellectual component of teaching, summed up in the idea of curriculum making. Over half the book explores how over 200 teachers of various subjects (across three schools) respond to the simple yet radical idea that what we teach young people should *empower* them. Obviously, the book in no sense offers a final word. But it does open up this question and provides productive ways to work with it.

David Lambert, Emeritus Professor of Geography Education, UCL Institute of Education, and co-author of *Race, Racism and the Geography Curriculum*

RICHARD BUSTIN

WHAT ARE WE TEACHING?

POWERFUL
KNOWLEDGE
AND A
CAPABILITIES
CURRICULUM

Crown House Publishing Limited
www.crownhouse.co.uk

First published by

Crown House Publishing Ltd

Crown Buildings, Bancyfelin, Carmarthen, Wales, SA33 5ND, UK

www.crownhouse.co.uk

and

Crown House Publishing Company LLC

PO Box 2223

Williston, VT 05495, USA

www.crownhousepublishing.com

British Library of Cataloguing-in-Publication Data

A catalogue entry for this book is available from the British Library.

Print ISBN: 9781785837180
Mobi ISBN: 9781785837333
ePub ISBN: 9781785837340
ePDF ISBN: 9781785837357

LCCN 2024940065

Printed in the UK by
Gomer Press Llandysul, Ceredigion

Foreword by Mary Myatt

The development of the curriculum is an ongoing professional endeavour, a never-ending story. *What are we Teaching?* is an important contribution to the professional conversations about what counts as a thoughtful curriculum, worthy of all the young people we teach.

Creating a curriculum is a source of endless fascination. It is crucial work; it is what schools 'do' and the debates about what is worth teaching and why are important. For these reasons, Richard Bustin's question – 'How can the nature of powerful knowledge in different school subjects be characterised?' – provides us with a fresh lens to consider the value and impact of curriculum development. *What are we Teaching?* offers some original research to help address that question. It is both robust and accessible in equal measure, quite a feat!

The inclusion and critique of narratives about the curriculum from across different, and sometimes opposing, positions is illuminating. As a result, Richard has provided us with an opportunity to scope the landscape and to consider alternative points of view. This is helpful for the reader as it sets out the background into which the fresh perspectives can be inserted. As Christine Counsell has argued, background knowledge is essential for pupils when learning new material: similarly, providing the reader with an overview is helpful for us as professionals, if we are to get to grips with the sometimes contested, yet fascinating, landscape of curricular models.

Drawing on wide-ranging research, including that of David Lambert and Michael Young, Richard argues that it is essential to honour the rigour of the individual subject domains, whilst at the same time foregrounding the subjects' potential for human development. In the analysis and critique of the Future curriculum scenarios, *What are we Teaching?* helps our own insights grow on two counts: we are reminded of the ways in which 'powerful knowledge' might be framed and we are also invited to distil meaning from each the elements that are likely to make most difference in teaching the individual subjects.

Richard shows us that the ways in which school subjects come to be framed and articulated are not the same for all disciplines. Whilst science and mathematics might bear a close relationship to the 'parent' academic field, this is less clear cut in some of the arts and humanities.

In presenting us with the alternative arguments, the terrain becomes very interesting. The elements that are currently thought to be most fruitful in terms of being worthy of inclusion in the curriculum are contested, quite rightly, over time. This is seen in the debates about the merits of texts selected in English, and the emerging calls for a wider range of diverse voices to be included in history and geography, for example.

What brings this book to life and what will make it so helpful for colleagues grappling with these important themes in schools, is that the work is informed by Richard's own research, both for his doctorate and for the purposes of this book. This is a remarkable bridge between the academic and the practical, 'work in progress' nature of curriculum debates in schools. *What are we Teaching?* considers the contested notion of powerful knowledge across the full range of school subjects and comes to some surprising conclusions. The book involves the voices of teachers from the three case study schools who spent time and energy exploring these ideas for themselves.

I was particularly struck by the inclusion of Amartya Sen's work as a way of framing the subjects as providing the space for developing capabilities. While Sen's work has, for the most part, been influential in geography curriculum development, it has the potential to inform discussions and insights in other subjects as well. The capabilities lens helps to take us beyond the examination specifications, important as these are, to the bigger capacity that each subject has for developing the human alongside the intellectual and academic capabilities of young people.

This book is a highly stimulating, thought-provoking, yet accessible read. Richard carries his scholarship lightly. He is ultimately practical in the way in which he takes us through the landscape, makes his arguments and poses questions for discussion and reflection at the end of each chapter. To articulate what powerful knowledge might be, in its most expansive sense, across each of the subjects is a truly remarkable piece of work. As such it will be immensely helpful to colleagues refining and upgrading their curriculum.

Mary Myatt, education advisor, writer, speaker and author

Acknowledgements

This book is over a decade in the making and, as such, I wish to thank a number of people whose thoughts and advice have helped me to shape the arguments you are about to read.

First is Professor David Lambert. David supervised my doctoral research whilst I was a part-time student at the UCL Institute of Education (and working as a full-time teacher). David's work on powerful knowledge and GeoCapabilities, as well as much of his collaborative work with others, is referenced throughout this book, and he invited me to take part in the GeoCapabilities 2 project. For this, and for his continued support since the completion of my doctoral research, I will always be very grateful. Thank you.

Secondly, I would like to thank the teachers whose words are featured in the second part of this book. They took part in the workshops as part of continuing professional development provision, knowing that I might use their responses somehow. They are anonymised, in line with research ethics, but they know who they are, and their contributions add a sense of realism to the ideas in the book.

I have had the pleasure of sharing many of these ideas with trainee and experienced teachers throughout the world and want to thank them for their engagement in discussions which have helped to shape my thinking. My own students in the schools where I have taught have helped to keep all these ideas grounded, and so they deserve my thanks too.

I also want to thank a small number of friends and colleagues who offered comments on earlier draft chapters: Dr Laura Barritt, Melody Bridges, Dr Cosette Crisan and Dr Arjan Reesink. I am honoured that Mary Myatt agreed to write the foreword to this book and want to thank her for her endorsement.

Finally, I want to thank my family – Sarah, Lizzie and Evie – for ensuring that I always had something more important to do than writing!

Contents

? Introduction

Have we lost our way?

According to Māori oral tradition, the goddess Hine Hukatere spent her days walking New Zealand's Southern Alps. One day she decided to visit the beach where she met and fell in love with the great warrior, Wawe. She invited Wawe back to her mountain home but as they hiked together, he could not keep up and he stumbled. An avalanche struck, and he disappeared forever. Hine Hukatere was distraught and began crying. She cried so much that Ranginui, the Sky Father, took pity on her and turned her tears into rivers of ice.

This story was told to me by a mountain guide as I stood gazing at the awesome glacial landscape that spread before me. I was on a geography field trip with my fellow undergraduates, and we were there to study the landscapes formed by ice in this spectacular mountain range in New Zealand. We were looking at Kā Roimata o Hine Hukatere: the frozen tears of Hine Hukatere. The names Franz Joseph Glacier and Fox Glacier as the two main glaciers in this part of the Southern Alps are more commonly known, came later when Europeans first set eyes on the landscape. Having told us this epic, tragic story, our guide rather dismissively proclaimed that we were there to study the causation of the glacier as we now know it. What followed was a rather more familiar story of snowfall, accumulation, glacier flow, erosional processes and the various scientific rigmarole of glacier function.

What struck me most was that the two stories of glacier formation were explained almost as if they were in conflict with each other and we had to choose which one we believed. We had to decide whether the glacier was formed by the frozen tears of a grief-stricken goddess or from the scientific processes of ice accumulation and flow. It was made clear to me on the day which one I needed to engage with, certainly as far as any essays were concerned. Yet, to me, pitching them against each other as claims to truth was misguided. Science, by which here (and in this book) I mean the methodological process of seeking reproducible truths, clearly was going to favour one story of glacier formation. Given that glaciers are found all over the world, the same set of processes can be observed, and the rigorous study of them furthers scientific understanding. But the Māori version of events is a different form of truth. It binds the mountains and the glaciers to the people who live there. The environment becomes inextricably linked to their being, through art, stories, music and culture. As such, the people have an in-built responsibility towards, and stewardship of, the environment; the mountains are not something 'othered', to be studied objectively, but are part of their very selves. It tells us more about the Māori people, their culture and their sustainable relationship with their landscape than any scientific mission could. The question is not which knowledge is better, but in what ways the knowledge(s) can help us to understand the world.

Many years later, I became a secondary school geography teacher and had the privilege of teaching glaciation to my own students. I will often start the first lesson by telling the story of Hine Hukatere, usually accompanied by a Google Earth fly-through of the Southern Alps on the interactive whiteboard. I hope this captures the students' imagination, gets them to engage with the landscape and begins to introduce the idea of how people treat the world around them. Given the headlines about retreating glaciers around the world as a result of climate change, understanding how people treat or mistreat the natural world is of contemporary relevance. Yet this is not how glaciation is approached in most textbooks. It is presented as a single story of scientific fact, devoid of human experience and interpretation. Students are required to learn the facts, draw the diagrams and sit the exam.

We seem to have lost our way

In the last few years, I have started to work more and more with trainee teachers. When I speak to groups towards the start of their training, they are still full of hope and big dreams. I ask them why they want to be teachers. They will often evoke ideas about wanting to make a difference, to challenge and change students' ideas about the major issues of the day, such as inequality. When I visit in the summer term towards the end of their training year, I often get a different response. By then, they will usually have had stints working in schools every day and mixing with teachers in real staffrooms. The answer to the same question then is usually about getting students through their exams, with talk of 'successful outcomes', getting them good enough results to go to college or wherever they want to go next. Many seem to have lost the big picture, the big motivation that probably compelled them to be a teacher in the first place.

I remember meeting one trainee teacher who was planning a lesson on migration. Before he went into detail about what he was going to do in the lesson, I asked him why he was teaching it. I was hoping that I might get an answer about the significance of migration in shaping modern society, or something about the migration stories that were in the news at the time. He was slightly flustered by my question and then said, 'Because that is the next lesson in the sequence.' I pushed him further, to really think why a lesson on migration might be significant in some way for the students. He stared at me intently and then said in an impassioned voice, 'Because it is really important the students know the difference between assessment objective 1 and assessment objective 2.'

He had become conditioned by exam speak and had not even finished his training year yet. Whilst this may well be the reality in many schools, a key contention in this book is that the over-tight grip of measurable exam results has stifled curriculum creativity in schools and diminished the student experience.

Choose your team: the traditionalists vs the progressives

When I first joined social media, displaying my job title of 'teacher', I was often asked if I was a traditionalist or a progressive. It was as if I had to choose my (online) team. The traditionalists were keen to maintain rigid subject boundaries and see children learn and recite facts; they would speak of educational ideals such as scholarship and rigour. The progressives, on the other hand, were much more interested in children's holistic development, nurtured through a creative curriculum with lots of interdisciplinary learning, the breakdown of subject boundaries and broad values such as personalised learning.

The problem for me is, at their extremes, both of these versions of education are found lacking. A focus purely on subjects for the sake of learning facts and taking exams never helps young people to develop the broader range of skills and competencies needed in the modern world. Yet remove the subjects completely – or dilute them so they simply become a means to another end – and something of real value is lost. As a geography teacher, the value of my subject is not in whether a young person can label all the world's oceans or know the name of the largest waterfall in the world.[1] There is something much more fundamental about geographical knowledge – and its importance for young people in the modern world, which goes well beyond listing facts to pass an exam – and that is why I became a geography teacher. Whilst I see the need to sit exams, the idea of teaching to the test in silent classrooms is not why I went into the profession. I do not feel that I'm a traditionalist, but do value the role of my subject, so I also feel far away from the most progressive arguments. In that sense, I have never had a team to join.

Making a compelling argument against the role of a subject curriculum, Michael Reiss and John White (2013) argue for an 'aims-based curriculum', placing the needs of the child, rather than subjects, at the centre of a curriculum. For them,

. . . .

school education should equip every child:

1. to lead a life that is personally flourishing

2. to help others to do so too. (Reiss and White, 2013: 4)

. . . .

To achieve this, knowledge is reframed as 'broad background understanding' (Reiss and White, 2013: 9) and there is a focus on interdisciplinary thinking, a breaking down of subject barriers, moral education and citizenship.

Those who argue for progressive education such as this tend not to have much to say about subjects. Often, they are seen as a problem, getting in the way of what is really valuable in education. Subjects become vehicles to achieve other educational goals. There is a lot of interdisciplinary exploration between subjects. Teaching progressively involves more

---

1   Even this is not straightforward. The highest waterfall in the world is Angel Falls (Kerepakupai Vená) in Venezuela, falling 979m (according to National Geographic). Yet this is nothing compared to the Denmark Strait cataract waterfall, which flows underwater. Cold dense water sinks down through warmer water for over 3,000m.

active styles of learning, such as discovery learning, where children are set free to learn for themselves and are able to follow their own interests. The antithesis is the more traditional view of education, espoused by a subject-based curriculum. Knowledge within the school subjects takes the form of facts to learn. The more facts that can be learnt, the more progress has been made, and students are tested on what they can remember. The work of American educationist E. D. Hirsch is often cited in arguments supporting a traditional curriculum. His famous 1988 book, *Cultural Literacy: What Every American Needs to Know*, is filled with facts that students should be able to remember at each stage of schooling. Traditional pedagogy involves copying from the board or from a textbook, learning passages of text by rote with high levels of discipline and silent working. Traditional education conjures up the image of the Victorian schoolroom, with a large blackboard, and the teacher holding chalk and getting children to repeat and copy down facts.

Despite the arguments in favour of a child-centred, aims-based approach to schooling, subjects – and the knowledge they provide for young people – have continued to provide the structure of the school system. This position was emboldened in England through the Conservative government's 'knowledge turn' in education policy (as described in Chapman, 2021a) in the first decades of the twenty-first century.

But not all subjects are equal. The 'core' subjects of English, mathematics and science run through all stages of schooling and, in England, are compulsory for young people right up to the age of 16. Other subjects such as history, geography and languages are compulsory up to the age of 14, after which they can be studied if the student chooses to carry on with them. The English Baccalaureate (EBacc) attempted to ensure that students were studying a range of rigorous subjects to GCSE level, which would enable greater access to university courses. To gain the EBacc, students had to achieve passes in English, maths, science, a language and history or geography. Yet this leaves out the importance of creative subjects, such as art and drama, or those aimed at health and fitness, like physical education (PE).

There has been much talk of the prominence of science, technology, engineering and maths (STEM) subjects in education. Precisely which subjects fit in each of the various categories is debatable; many geographers are keen to claim that geography is a STEM subject. The acronym originated from the work of the National Science Foundation in the USA in 2001, and attempts to identify the subject areas that will lead to the greatest employability and income. The acronym has taken on a life of its own, with others adding 'A' (for arts) to make STEAM, yet this leaves the languages and humanities subjects out as if they are somehow second class and don't matter any more, despite their inclusion in the EBacc. Add into this talk of more vocational choices post-16, instead of traditional university routes, and you have a busy system with many options which can appear confusing.

If both traditionalist and progressive approaches to curriculum have their merits, then it is time to move on from this simple dualism. Even schools that claim to be progressive will often have passionate subject specialists teaching subject knowledge. Schools that are traditional on the face of it often have a wide-ranging programme of additional activities and extracurricular arts education. Knowledge is a component of both progressive and traditional models of education, although what sort of knowledge, whose knowledge and how it is derived clearly differs.

The work of Guy Claxton has been particularly influential in education, and he too has moved debates beyond the traditionalist–progressive dichotomy in curriculum thinking. In *The Learning Power Approach: Teaching Learners to Teach Themselves* (2018), he discusses a range of techniques derived from cognitive science. His work takes curriculum debates beyond an antagonism between simply learning facts to pass exams (the traditionalist position) or nurturing student wellbeing (a more progressive position) to look at how students learn, and how an understanding of this can help young people to develop and achieve. Yet he writes less about the place of school subjects within this framework. His work seems to suggest that subjects do exist and are part of the structured organisation of schools, but the reasons for this – and the benefits this might bring – are less well discussed. Even if we have a clear understanding of why we went into teaching, and we have found a school where our own ideologies align with the institutional values, there is a further complication when it comes to deciding what we are teaching. As far back as 2007, the independent think tank Civitas produced a report into the school curriculum. In a press release, they argued:

. . . .

The traditional subject areas have been hi-jacked to promote fashionable causes such as gender awareness, the environment and anti-racism, while teachers are expected to help to achieve the government's social goals instead of imparting a body of academic knowledge to their students. (Civitas, 2007)

. . . .

They describe this as the 'corruption of the curriculum' and devoted a full-length book to their concerns in a 2007 publication of the same name (edited by Robert Whelan). In this book, a range of writers describe how pressures have conspired to influence the nature of what is being taught in schools. Much of what they describe foresaw some curricular and cultural battlegrounds in the decades to come. As Frank Furedi (2007: 1) identifies in the introduction, 'Everyone with a fashionable cause wants a piece of the curriculum.' The writers then show how a range of traditional subjects have in some way been subject to corrupting influences. Geography, according to Alex Standish (2007: 28), 'used to be about maps', but now has become a vehicle for environmentalism and multiculturalism, or what could loosely be described as the green left political agenda. Michele Ledda (2007: 18), in her chapter on English literature, argues:

> A British pupil can go through the school system and get the top marks in English and English Literature without knowing that Spenser, Milton or Pope ever existed, but having studied Carol Ann Duffy twice, both at GCSE and A-level. With all due respect to Carol Ann Duffy, she is on the syllabus, not because she is a greater poet than Milton, but because she is more 'relevant', dealing as she does with very contemporary issues such as disaffected learners.

I am sure teachers of English literature would have much to say about this, and we pick this story up again in Chapter 6. These disagreements about what we should be teaching in schools will be explored throughout this book.

Don't change the subject!

Curriculum is defined in many ways, but in this book it describes the grand thinking about what we choose to teach in schools and why. 'Curriculum' literally translates to 'race course': the idea being that it is something to be followed. It is different from the notion of 'pedagogy', which describes how a curriculum is enacted, how the teaching takes place to enable learning. The subjects on offer in any one school bear remarkable similarity to any other, and in the UK many follow the national curriculum. It has not always been this way. Which subjects are on offer to students is not somehow set in stone and is open to debate and discussion.

Educational sociologist David Layton (1972) identified the life cycle of a subject, in which a new subject starts out of a perceived need. The need could be based on student interest, advances in technology or political necessity. Citizenship was introduced in schools in England in 2002 as a means to teach students about democracy and voting, despite these topics being taught in history (and other humanities). Natural history is another new subject designed to teach climate change in a new way, despite climate science being a key part of geography and the science subjects for decades. As coding and artificial intelligence (AI) is proliferating in more areas of society, so the curriculum is responding; computer science is rapidly becoming one of the fastest growing A level options for students in the UK (BCS, 2022).

As new subjects become more established, they attract more scholarly work to develop their key organising principles. This strengthens links to university disciplines and enables teachers to be trained as specialists. Examination courses and teacher continuing professional development (CPD) might be offered. A professional subject association is created which helps unify and regulate the knowledge in the subject, and this body provides further support and training for teachers. Once established, however, subjects can be lost from the curriculum. They can merge with other subjects or see reduced curriculum time as other new subjects appear. Classical languages such as Latin used to be a key feature of curricula of the past but now are only really the preserve of independent schools. This is a story picked up in Chapter 10.

In his book *Trivium 21c: Preparing Young People for the Future with Lessons from the Past*, Martin Robinson (2013) explains how the school curriculum from classical times through to the Middle Ages focused on the trivium of grammar (or essential knowledge), dialectic (questioning and reasoning) and rhetoric (communicating ideas with confidence). He argues that refocusing on these ideals can offer a lot in contemporary curriculum debates.

The relationship between a school subject and the university discipline that shares its name is not straightforward. Ivor Goodson's (2005) work shows that sometimes the school subject predates the university discipline, with the latter being created initially to provide schools with well-trained specialist teachers.[2] For other school subjects, such as creative subjects, the aims and methods are very different to the academic discipline. Some school subjects do not have a university discipline at all, despite being on the curriculum for decades – such as personal, social, health and economic (PSHE) education.

Despite subjects being the basis of a school curriculum, and teachers employed as specialists, attempts are often made to break down subject barriers and to teach in a cross-curricular way. Sometimes this is done in a grand scale, off timetable, 'everyone in the hall with large pieces of sugar paper' sort of way, but equally it is often done over the course of a normal school week, with all teachers asked to teach a lesson around a central theme (such as 'the future' or 'togetherness'). There are often informal conversational links made between teachers too, such as English and art finding common ground to look together at the teaching of a particular idea. What is always important in an exercise like this is to understand the aim. Too often, the idea is to show students how unimportant subject boundaries are, and that when we break them down, we see how the world really is. What usually ends up being shown is the complete opposite. Each subject contributes to the central theme in a different way, and students can gain an understanding of exactly how that subject's knowledge is able to offer a particular insight. What science can tell us about a glacier is very different to what art – or English literature or folk knowledge – can tell us.

This book sets out to challenge teachers to explore why their subject is really important in an overcrowded curriculum. It sets out to explore how knowledge is constructed in different subjects and how this can be empowering for young people. This 'disciplined' thinking cannot be gained from progressive, unstructured 'pedagogic adventures' (as Lambert (2011) has described), nor from a reductive curriculum that boils subject knowledge down to a set of predictable exam questions. It builds on the work of Guy Claxton (2018), looking at how students learn within different subjects.

The curricular issues outlined here have occurred against a backdrop of material challenges facing the profession. The first is a recruitment crisis. According to reports in the *TES*, not enough new teachers are entering the profession each year (Martin, 2023) and, of those who do

---

2   Geography is an example of this. Even though the organised academic discipline is relatively new (e.g. the work of Halford Mackinder from the early twentieth century), the thought process of geography is much older. Geography can trace its intellectual roots back to ancient Greece.

train, a third leave the profession within five years of qualifying (Lough, 2020). There are many reasons for these recruitment issues, and exploring these would take a whole other book, but I cannot help but wonder if this obsession we seem to have with exam results and measurable outputs puts undue pressure on teachers. Instead of educating the young people in their care, they must ensure that students are jumping through a set of predetermined societal hoops. Secondly, teachers are not trusted any more. More and more planning is done centrally and pushed out to teachers in schools who then have to 'deliver' the material uncritically to their students. This takes away the autonomy to decide what they want to teach, how and why. This is a deprofessionalisation that potentially allows for more non-qualified teachers to enter the classroom to deliver set packages.

Schools, and by extension therefore teachers, have far too many expectations placed upon them. Teachers are expected to get students through examinations *and* act as social workers and, increasingly, parents, by taking on roles that were traditionally their preserve. All that as well as trying to ensure that students leave school with confidence and resilience.

A far more ambitious way of thinking about what we teach and why is through the notion of capabilities, from the work of Amartya Sen (1980), Martha Nussbaum (2006) and Melanie Walker (2006). This is explored fully in later chapters. They suggest that rather than judging the success of education on measurable outputs – for example, exam pass rates or inclusion data – we should instead be focusing on what a young person is able to do with the knowledge they have gained: how they think and how they interact with the world in new and creative ways. Expressed in this way it sounds like a classic description of a progressive curriculum, but work done through the GeoCapabilities projects – and that of David Lambert (e.g. Solem et al., 2013) – looked at the role that subject knowledge plays in developing capabilities. Subjects, through what Michael Young (2008) has described as 'powerful knowledge', can empower students to think in new ways. This idea is critiqued by some writers, which is explored further in Chapter 3.

This book has been created in conjunction with teachers, and it challenges teachers to explore what knowledge their subject teaches, and what powerful knowledge might mean for their subject, if anything. Specifically, the entire teaching staff from three UK secondary schools were asked to identify and express the ways in which their subject could be powerful knowledge for young people.

Part I explores the theoretical background to the ideas mentioned so far: types of knowledge, capabilities and the notion of curriculum. The research element, and what teachers had to say, is the focus of Part II.

For discussion

? Think back to when you first started teaching, or first wanted to teach. What was your motivation? Has that changed over time?

? Where would you place yourself within the traditionalist vs progressive debate?

? What role does your subject specialism play in your professional identity?

? Write down a list of qualities with which you think every young person should walk out of compulsory education. Now work backwards. How would you plan a school day for hundreds of children that would enable them to develop these qualities? How might subjects fit into this picture?

Part I: Theory

Introduction to Part I

This first part of the book explores a range of ideas that were alluded to in the introduction: the battle between a traditional and progressive view of curriculum; the status and nature of knowledge, skills and values in the curriculum; and powerful knowledge and capabilities as a means to move beyond some of the debates of the past.

Wider reading

In many ways, this book in the latest in a long line of texts which help teachers and leaders get to grips with the complexities of curriculum. Mary Myatt's (2018) *The Curriculum: Gallimaufry to Coherence* is a wide-ranging text telling the story of the changing nature of curriculum and the importance of subjects within it. Her accessible storytelling makes this a great introduction to a wide range of curriculum issues. Ruth Ashbee's (2021) *Curriculum: Theory, Culture and the Subject Specialisms* is slightly more academic in nature and focuses on the knowledge implicit in a range of subjects which are presented in the form of visual diagrams. Alka Sehgal Cuthbert and Alex Standish's (2021) edited collection, *What Should Schools Teach? Disciplines, Subjects and the Pursuit of Truth*, sees subject experts unpicking and exploring a range of ideas related to their own subjects, how notions of 'truth' can be ascertained and why this matters for teachers. *Knowledge and the Future School* by Michael Young and David Lambert (2014) was the first book to really explore ideas around powerful knowledge, a key idea in this book, and its links to curriculum thinking in schools. My own doctoral research (Bustin, 2017a) and follow-up book, *Geography Education's Potential and the Capability Approach: GeoCapabilities and Schools* (Bustin, 2019), made the case for a powerful-knowledge-led school geography curriculum, which was swiftly followed by Mark Enser's *Powerful Geography: A Curriculum with Purpose in Practice* (2021), which explores some practical implications of those ideas for geography teachers. Powerful knowledge in history education is explored in the wide-ranging *Knowing History in Schools: Powerful Knowledge and the Powers of Knowledge*, edited by Arthur Chapman (2021a).

What unites all these books is the idea that subjects sit at the heart of curriculum thinking and that they provide the best means for young people to access knowledge, skills and understanding. This book builds on the existing literature in a few key ways. Firstly, this is the first book to look at the contested notion of powerful knowledge across the full range of school subjects. As we will see, it may not always be the best framework with which to express the value of some subjects. Secondly, this book includes the voices of real teachers from three case study schools who have spent time and energy exploring these ideas for themselves. Their voices provide the stimulus for discussion in Part II. Finally, this book links powerful knowledge to the notion of the capability approach, and the conclusion begins to think about what students might be capable of thinking, being and doing with an empowering curriculum. The links between capabilities and curriculum have been explored in some key texts – Professor David Lambert's work has been particularly influential here (Lambert et al., 2015) – and this work builds on these previous discussions.

Conclusions

The first part of this book unpicks the theory behind the ideas. Chapters 1 and 2 discuss the status of 'knowledge' in schools, before the balance between knowledge and skills, and discussions around powerful knowledge, is unpicked in Chapter 3. Chapter 4 looks at the capability approach to curriculum thinking and how this is a broad and ambitious idea for schools. In the second part of the book, each chapter looks at a different subject, linking to the theory from the first part and exploring what it looks like in practice in schools. At the end of each chapter there is a series of questions designed to provoke further thought and discussion. These can be used for individual reflection, as well as forming the basis for group discussion.

Chapter 1

We've 'had enough of experts'

The infamous quote that forms the title of this chapter was uttered on British television on 3 June 2016 by a member of parliament and leading figure in politics, Michael Gove MP. Mr Gove had been secretary of state for education from 2010 to 2014 and was responsible for many reforms during his tenure, including what was later dubbed the 'knowledge turn' in education: a refocus on the importance of teaching discernible facts. The occasion was an interview on *Sky News* with presenter Faisal Islam in the run-up to the Brexit referendum on whether the UK should leave the European Union (EU). His outburst was in response to the challenge that economic experts had unilaterally warned against leaving the EU; Mr Gove was a key figure in the Leave campaign. His response was to suggest that 'the people in this country have had enough of experts from organisations with acronyms saying that they know what is best' (*Sky News*, 2016). What is more surprising looking back on this debate is the reaction from the live studio audience. Rather than recoiling in horror at the idea that a leading national figure would disparage the advice of experts in their field, they cheered him loudly. It was, to me, a live affirmation of a trend towards populist politics that was spreading across the UK, the USA and much of Europe. Politicians were saying what people wanted to hear, and both they and their audiences seemed oblivious to any voice of reason from experts. Opinions, whether or not they hold up against the available evidence, were given equal billing as claims for truth. So-called 'experts' were painted as being out of touch by an increasingly opportunistic media and political class.

It was not just economic forecasts that were rubbished by the media. Social media posts began to question basic scientific facts that had been proved long ago by meticulous scientific investigation. The most obvious of these which has come into question again in the twenty-first century is that the shape of the Earth is a sphere;[1] unlike some voices who try to convince us otherwise, the Earth is not flat.

Human civilisations have long questioned the shape of the Earth. The poet Homer, in c. eighth century BC, writes about a flat Earth, a view shared by many of the early Egyptian, Mesopotamian and Chinese civilisations. A popular myth is that belief in a flat Earth was maintained until only the last few hundred years when the enlightened Europeans were able to 'prove' it for the benefit of the rest of the world. The story goes that Christopher Columbus (1451–1506) was advised not to sail west out of Portugal to reach wealthy Cathay in the Far East (modern-day Northern China) as he risked falling off the end of the Earth. In fact, this myth was created by the author Washington Irving in his 1828 biography of Columbus. The myth perpetuates that it was not until Ferdinand Magellan's ship *Victoria* circumnavigated the world from 1519 to 1522 that there was final proof that the Earth was, indeed, a globe. This is simply not true; it is a Eurocentric spin on history. The chances are that Columbus was well aware of the shape of the Earth. This retelling of history to create a positive European narrative happens quite a lot it seems.

The ancient Greeks were some of the first to study 'geodesy': the size, shape, position and gravitational effects of the Earth in space. Followers of the work of Pythagoras, in the sixth century BC, observed that the moon and the sun were spheres and that the Earth was therefore likely to follow the same shape, and this would give us day and night – an idea supported by philosophers such as Plato and Aristotle. There were some who thought that the Earth stood still and the heavens rotated, but it was the work of Eratosthenes in the third century BC that really pushed on the science of geodesy. He calculated the circumference of the Earth to remarkable accuracy. Exact details seem to vary, but according to an article published in the journal *Science* (King-Hele, 1976), Eratosthenes was working in Aswan in modern-day Egypt and identified that the sun was directly overhead at midsummer, shining right down a vertically dug well. Almost due north of there, at Alexandria, he used a stick to identify that the sun was 7.2 degrees away from the vertical at the same time. He measured the distance between the two places by timing how long it took a camel to walk between them and using its average pace to calculate the distance. He used mathematics to then work out that the circumference of the Earth must be fifty times the distance between Aswan and Alexandria. If the Earth were a sphere, then by his reckoning,

---

1   Actually, it would be more correct to call it an oblate spheroid.

the equator must be 28,500 miles long. Modern equipment has meas-ured it to be 24,500 miles. By the first century BC, the Earth being a globe was an uncontroversial truth. The flattening of the Earth at the poles was proposed by Sir Isaac Newton in *Principia* (published in 1687), and in the twentieth century space flight enabled astronauts to take photographs and to measure with accuracy elements of modern geodesy.

Despite the considerable evidence to the contrary, held true for centu-ries, there are still people who believe that the Earth is flat. The International Flat Earth Society was founded in 1956 by Samuel Shenton, a fellow of both the Royal Geographical Society and the Royal Astronomical Society. Membership of the Flat Earth Society has increased over the last decade and it held its first ever international con-ference as recently as 2017. Many of its members might well have joined out of curiosity rather than a deep-held belief but, nonetheless, flat earth is big business, and the cunning use of social media, the disparaging of experts and the ease with which people question and challenge long-held facts has helped to ensure their views can be spread widely.

We live in an era of fake news. Plausible stories are created, a suitable image is found to accompany it, an enticing clickbait headline is given and then the story is put on the internet. It can be read and shared hun-dreds or thousands of times before any effort is made to correct it. Even if the post gets deleted and some form of apology issued, it is too late. The story is out and will forever be part of the folklore of that topic. There have always been conspiracy theorists willing to twist truths, but it has never been so easy to spread disinformation online. This provides a con-siderable challenge for teachers in schools.

There is a further challenge. Celebrities with a large public profile are often given airtime on TV or radio to speak about subjects on which they have no knowledge or experience. We listen to them because they have achieved success in other domains of public life. In recent years, we have had to endure footballer Gary Neville giving us his views on schooling and singer Charlotte Church explaining her vision for education. Celebrities using their profile to raise awareness for a charitable cause is one thing, but taking up valuable airtime to lecture on a topic they clearly know nothing about beyond the superficial is quite another. When expert educational leaders are invited on to programmes, they are not given time to speak about football or classical singing, yet somehow it is OK the other way round.

Why has this happened?

Conspiracy theories have always existed, but these ideas seem to have become more mainstream in the past few decades. The blame, according to Eli Pariser in his 2011 book *The Filter Bubble*, lies with the internet and the use of social media. Not only does social media enable people with niche interests to connect, but it is also a key source of news for many people. In December 2009, Google introduced an algorithm which changed the way in which its search results were shown to consumers (Pariser, 2011b). Versions of this have been introduced across social media platforms since then. If a user clicks on a link, an algorithm buried in the site records the interaction and automatically offers more of the same content to users in future. This is done at the expense of other types of content. So, if a particular user clicks on a link to an article about the COVID-19 vaccine being used to inject data-harvesting technology, then the next time they use the same device to conduct a similar search, they will see similar content appearing. Repeated clicks on these types of articles will tell the algorithm that this is the sort of content the user wants, and it will keep offering them more. This algorithm was initially introduced without consumer knowledge, but even now it can lead to confirmation bias – the idea that a particular view can be reinforced time and time again through repeated clicks in the backwaters of the internet. The user wallows within their own online filter bubble, not always realis-ing that their social media platform is filtering out content on their behalf. Those who view this content become more and more convinced that what they are reading is mainstream, so it is no wonder they believe that experts have got it wrong. The internet offers a blog written in some-one's bedroom which is riddled with factual errors alongside a peer reviewed piece of academic writing, and the consumer might be none the wiser about which has a greater claim to factual correctness. Nor might they care.

The COVID-19 lockdowns made the impact of online filter bubbles much worse. With conferences and meetings cancelled, urgent business was conducted online. Whilst ruthlessly efficient, what was missing was the opportunity for people to talk and interact socially, disagree and shape each other's opinions about all sorts of topics. Under normal circumstances, interacting with other people will usually alert someone to the fact that they have been down an online rabbit hole and this will challenge them to rethink, to specifically seek alternative reading material. These encounters did not happen, and instead people retreated into their online filter bubbles. The mute and block functions of social media also mean that people are easily able to take out any voice that does not agree with theirs. Indeed, it seems to be a badge of honour for some to declare proudly that they no longer follow someone who disagrees with them. It means people shout into an online echo chamber, getting increasingly incensed at the world, convinced they are correct and finding multiple – if niche and dubious – sources of information to corroborate their view of the world.

We have, it seems, had enough of experts and are happy to wallow in the comfort of echo chambers that repeat what we want to hear. This makes us less tolerant of the experts who might want to challenge our thinking. We have pressed a societal mute button, protecting our ears from their expertise.

What is the impact for teachers in schools?

I put online filter bubbles to the test with a group of trainee teachers. It was June 2022, and the trainees were at the end of their school placements but still completing their final weeks of university-based training. As part of a session I was running on capabilities and classroom knowledge (the themes in this book), I got the trainees to open up a web browser on their usual device and type two words into their usual search engine: 'migration' and 'Rwanda'. The British Conservative government had recently introduced a policy to fly asylum claimants to Rwanda for processing and this was a major news story at the time. It was also the month of Queen Elizabeth's Platinum Jubilee celebrations. Prince Charles, then heir to the British throne, had been overheard making a comment about the Rwanda policy which was reported in a number of newspapers in the preceding weeks. This was frowned upon; members of the royal family are unelected and meant to stay out of politics.

When looking at the search results that appeared on each of their screens, the trainees started to compare and contrast how their search engines had selected material for them based on their usual online behaviour. What was astonishing to them was how different they were. Most trainees did not have any reference to the royal family on the first page of results. One trainee had an article on Prince Charles as the third suggestion. She then admitted that she had recently been searching for materials connected to the royal family. If that teacher had been preparing materials for a lesson on migration, the Prince Charles comments may well have made an appearance given how far up in the results the article appeared, whereas this was unlikely for the other teachers in the room.

The anti-intellectualist populism that has spread throughout much of the world in the early decades of the twenty-first century has real implications for teachers in schools. Not only is there a need to help students discern fact from fiction – and perhaps, more interestingly, to help them understand why certain fictions are more persuasive than the actual facts – but also teachers themselves need to keep up to date with the latest thinking in their subject specialism and in education more broadly. As teachers, we are not immune to disappearing into an online filter bubble and believing the hype.

The need for expert teachers

Teachers need to be the experts in the classroom. They need to be experts in the subject they are teaching. As we will see in the next chapter, this is about more than just being a few pages ahead in the textbook but having a deep grounding in the subject and understanding how knowledge is created and how claims of truth can be made. Primary (elementary) school teachers have a greater task here as they need to be experts in a variety of subjects, and understanding the essence of each subject is key. Teachers also need to be education experts. This is not just something gained from experience – important though this is – but from an understanding of how children learn best; by asking curricular and pedagogical questions about what we choose to teach and why. This is the reason why teaching remains, for the moment at least, a graduate profession.

Students arrive in our classrooms with the beginnings of a political identity. Their ideas will be shaped by their parents initially, as students will often repeat phrases they have heard at home when discussing contemporary issues. Our role is to challenge their views, gently encouraging them to back up their claims with evidence, then questioning where that evidence has come from and how reliable it is. Students are allowed to change their minds, and the classroom is a safe space where they can explore ideas and differing viewpoints, seeing the limitations in what they read and the media they consume.

That is much easier to say than it is to do in practice, of course. Students who are overtly racist, sexist or homophobic absolutely need to be robustly challenged. Those who make claims that are simply not correct – such as, 'the Earth is flat' – need equal challenge. Yet there are other ideas that are open to debate, such as what meaning can be gleaned from a piece of art or drama. It is what some in the literature (e.g. Tubb, 2003) have dubbed as the difference between 'public values' – to which all society subscribes – and 'non-public values' – where there are levels of nuance and debate. Our role as teachers is to inculcate public values and clarify the debate within non-public values, so that students can decide where they stand on issues for themselves. Yet nowhere is there a list of what these public and non-public values are. The Department for Education (2014) produced a list of 'British values' that all teachers need to be actively promoting, which included ideas such as mutual respect and tolerance of people of different faiths, the rule of law and democracy. Yet even this is contested; quite why these are 'British' as opposed to universal values has never been explained. Some of the important work currently being done by those interested in decolonising the curriculum is challenging the origins of many of these British values. For some teachers, public values can be presented to students as a debate; for others, non-public values are taught as a given. Without any clearer guidance, this will always be a source of argument between teachers and those who have an interest in education, and this can lead back to claims of curricular corruption.

Student expertise

Our students do not grow up in an information vacuum. They too are avid consumers of knowledge, a source of which for many is social media. A report from Ofcom (2022) identified the top three news sources as Instagram, TikTok and YouTube, with 29%, 28% and 28% of young people (aged 12–15) using these respectively. Given the more recent proliferation of sites like ChatGPT, AI is likely to be the dominating information source of the future. Even if we can persuade students to pick up a newspaper or to read news stories online, there are still the challenges of bias. A YouGov poll in 2017 (Smith, 2017) asked respondents to identify bias in UK media outputs. The survey identified a left-wing bias for *The Guardian*

(71% of those asked said it was slightly, fairly or very left wing) and a right-wing bias for the *Daily Mail* (81% of those surveyed said it was slightly, fairly or very right wing), with others, such as *The Independent*, *The Times* and *The Telegraph* placed somewhere in between. An article in the *Daily Mail* will take a very different stance on an issue to the same story in *The Guardian*. As a geography teacher, I used to collect news clippings for a wall display called 'geography in the news'. It was designed so that my students could see the real-world relevance of what I was teaching them. Yet it struck me once that nearly all the clippings on my display were from *The Guardian*. The 'left-leaning' paper (as the YouGov poll identifies) tends to report more on the environmental and climate stories that I was teaching. Many issues, such as rising sea levels and human displacement due to climate change, were simply not being covered by the more right-wing press. It is no wonder that the ways in which school geography is taught in schools have been accused of 'corruption', with students and teachers taking uncritical stances on ideas like environmentalism (e.g. Standish, 2007).

The growing inaccessibility of science

The above set of arguments presents a bleak picture for the nature of knowledge and claims of 'truth' in schools. Yet our role as teachers must be to help our students to uncover facts, separate truth from opinion and news from fake news. We also need to keep up with the latest knowledge from both our subject specialisms and the field of education, without which it is difficult to consider ourselves experts.

The peer review system of academic publication is still the best means we have developed as a society to ensure the reliability of factual knowledge. Academics conduct research according to the rules and norms of their subject discipline (more on this process for each subject is discussed in Part II), write this up and submit it to a journal, of which there are many. Their article is then sent around to fellow academics with expertise in the topic being researched who offer their thoughts and comments, which the author can respond to before it is then published and contributes to 'knowledge' in that particular field. Yet even this process is not perfect. Firstly, the research that is conducted in the first place is the product of funding. Some research topics, such as boys' underachievement in education studies, might receive more funding than others, such as classroom layout. Thus, the more popular and trendy the topic, the more funding it receives. The process of finding 'peers' is also challenging. Some fields of knowledge are very small, so finding people to review papers can be problematic.

As some of the recent voices arguing for decolonising the curriculum have outlined, some of the norms and values that have developed over time within subject disciplines are themselves steeped in power relation-ships. For example, for many decades geographers have created a series of conceptual models to explain the world, such as the famous Burgess model of urban areas (Park and Burgess, 1925). This is a diagram of con-centric circles, which sees the central business district represented in the centre, surrounded by rings of factories, then low-class housing, middle-class housing and then suburban housing. This simplification was an attempt to make sense of land use in cities, but it silences the people who live and interact in those spaces and lumps diverse groups of people together, making assumptions about class in the process. This whole way of 'doing geography', repeated across a range of other models from the time, can be viewed as an expression of power: silencing and classifying diverse groups of cultural minorities. This particular model was based on 1920s industrial Chicago, and whilst geographers went on to find new ways to make sense of urban spaces from the 1970s onwards, the Burgess model still features in school geography textbooks as a way of trying to describe modern cities. If and how the model should be used has been the topic of recent debate for geography teachers (e.g. Rawding, 2019; Puttick, 2020).

There is a further challenge in accessing peer reviewed knowledge. Donald P. Hayes' famous 1992 paper 'The growing inaccessibility of sci-ence' was published in the prestigious journal *Nature*. In it he reported how lots of great research was being done across a range of fields, but the articles were all hidden behind paywalls, thereby rendering them inac-cessible to a wider public or even a professional audience. At least, I think that is what it is about. The irony is that the publisher charges anyone who wants to view it $8.99 for the article or $199 for a year's subscription to the journal.

Students in schools do not read peer reviewed articles, except perhaps in the final years as they get ready for university. But as teachers, peer reviewed, reliable, research-based data is the most reliable source of updates to our subject and pedagogical knowledge. Yet, unless a teacher is enrolled in some form of further study at a university or has a subscription to a subject association, access to this vital knowledge becomes unobtainable.[2]

Different subjects will require different levels of engagement with the parent academic discipline studied at universities. The discourse of some subjects changes rapidly; those who teach politics probably have the most difficult challenge keeping their knowledge up to date. Other subjects change more slowly; those who teach Classics may well find the pace of change in the discourse is slower. I am not suggesting for one moment that the contemporary discourse of Classics is somehow settled – it is as vibrant as any other discipline with a range of journals. But for teachers in schools who are introducing classical languages to students, the rate of engagement with the parent discipline will be less than in other subjects. As we will see in Part II, some subject communities would even question whether there is a relationship between the parent academic discipline and its school existence.

Despite varying engagement with the parent discipline, education itself is a vibrant academic discourse. Recent discussions have revolved around an increasing application of principles from cognitive science to classroom practice (e.g. Willingham, 2021) and efforts to decolonise the curriculum, as well as, of course, the role of knowledge in the curriculum, to which this book contributes. These recent discussions have helped to re-professionalise teaching, the irony being that trainee teachers will engage with these ideas as part of their training but, once in the classroom, will have very little opportunity to access journals to push their professional knowledge further. Some classroom teachers will have read no original educational theory since they trained. Ideas that were once common parlance, such as the VAK model of learning styles (which states that all learners are either visual, auditory or kinaesthetic and therefore we should alter our teaching to accommodate each style) has been shown to not be based in any form of evidence. It is just not true. It is fake educational news, yet it was taught prolifically on teacher training programmes in the 2000s and still seems to crop up now and again at conferences.

One source of knowledge that is accessible to all is the blog. Many teachers have set up pages to post advice, share resources, give opinions and discuss educational issues. Readers are able to comment on and share these posts. On the one hand, this is the ultimate form of educational

---

2   I write this fully in the knowledge that I edit a journal for teachers that is stuck behind a paywall. Access is via subscription through the Geographical Association (the subject association for geography teachers).

knowledge sharing. There are no pay walls; everyone has equal access. There is also the ultimate peer review process – teachers, by commenting, liking and sharing the blog posts, are able to add value. Those who post untruths are soon found out as comments will point out the error of the author's ways. Sometimes this leads to the writer redrafting the post or adding another to update their thinking. It is almost a live peer review process. Yet relying on blogging rather than academically peer reviewed material is problematic. Firstly, whose blogs get read and shared most is often more a product of who has the biggest following, perhaps those who have a lot to say or who share teaching resources rather than those who have done any original research themselves. Often, fake news is presented as fact and not checked. Another blogger might then pick up and discuss the idea, and so the mistruth is spread further. A 'peer' in the peer review process is someone who has specific knowledge on the topic, not simply another person in the same job, so relying on lots of fellow teachers reading and commenting will not provide the same function.

I spent much of my doctorate studying powerful knowledge, which I discuss in Chapter 3 of this book. It is an idea which is easily misunderstood, and many blog posts cropped up at the end of the 2010s discussing it incorrectly. Further bloggers spread this information and I suddenly found myself trying to 'police' social media, (politely) correcting people who had got it wrong and linking them to some of the original work that explains the concept accurately. It soon became an impossible task.

Conclusions: have we really had enough of experts?

There is a further challenge to ensuring that teachers are 'experts'. The centre of gravity in teacher training is shifting away from university schools of education to schools themselves. For those trained as part of school-based and 'apprentice' programmes, the emphasis is much more on practical classroom experience rather than the theoretical underpinnings of the discourse. Thus, the opportunities to engage with the discipline are varied. These teachers may soon be in leadership roles in schools, responsible for training and developing other teachers.

Teachers do get opportunities to engage with the latest ideas without reading peer reviewed journal articles. Schools and multi-academy trusts all provide ongoing professional training which is usually based on the latest ideas. There has also been the rise of the teacher writer – teachers writing books and blogs for other teachers full of experience and advice, but sometimes lacking a critical stance on the ideas discussed.

A lack of opportunity for teachers to access high-quality research has coincided with a changing professional teacher training climate. Teachers need to access quality material more than ever. If we wish to remain professional and research-led, we need to be able to access and contribute to expert knowledge. This has become increasingly difficult in recent years.

For discussion

? Show your students Eli Pariser's (2011a) TED talk which illustrates the significance of online algorithms. (Pariser is also the author of *The Filter Bubble* (2011b).) Discuss the extent to which this could have implications for the way in which you teach your lessons or the ways in which students might access information.

? Find a news story that relates in some way to what you teach in the classroom. How is it reported in *The Guardian* and in the *Daily Mail*. Can your students pick up on the nuances of language? Is there a particular emphasis that one news outlet takes over another?

? In a group, open a search engine on the devices that you each normally use. Type in the same word or pair of words. Compare the web pages that are offered to each group member. Try to think about what might account for the differences and how this might impact your lesson preparation. If you have access to an AI chatbot (like ChatGPT), ask that too.

Chapter 2

Why are we doing this?

Knowledge and truth

I show my students a photograph of James Hutton (1726–1797) towards the start of their geography course. He has been called the 'father of modern geology'; his work was truly ground-breaking. He studied a variety of rock formations in Scotland and argued against prevailing theories about the age of the Earth. In 1650, Bishop Usher had calculated that, according to the Bible, the Earth was created in 4,004 BC. Hutton is credited with introducing the notion of deep time and the geological timeline. He also argued that the Earth is not static but the product of a series of land and marine processes: rock formations now visible on the Earth's surface originated from processes that took place under the oceans. This opposed the mainstream view that the land as we now see it was the product of the great flood in the Bible. His ideas were visionary, and later scientists, including Charles Lyell and Charles Darwin, cite Hutton's work as an influence on their thinking.

Yet I point out to my students that if they understand that the Earth's crust is divided into a series of tectonic plates which move slowly around the globe and that it is this movement which can create mountains, volcanoes and earthquakes, which contribute to the rock cycle, then they already know more geology than James Hutton ever knew in his lifetime.[1] The content of one term of work in a school geography classroom will provide students with more knowledge than a famed geographer living a few hundred years ago ever had. This is progress; each successive generation knows more than the previous one.

---

1   The theory of continental drift is credited to the work of Alfred Wegener (1880–1930) some 150 years or so later.

Yet this process is not an ancient one. When I started teaching, the main-stream media and teaching press were still exercising caution over how we talk about climate change, despite the scientific consensus by that point clearly linking human activities to a change in the global climate. Now it is the climate deniers who occupy an increasingly small space on social media.

Even in the non-scientific fields, new knowledge is being created and new understanding about the world – and, by extension, ourselves – is being developed and challenged in equal measure through literature and art. Knowledge develops and changes over time; advances are still being made across all fields of human knowledge. Various journals chronicle the advances and challenges in our disciplines. Add to this the idea that, over the last century, increasing proportions of humanity have experienced a formal education, we have created what David Baker (2014) calls a global 'schooled society'. We should be living in the most knowledgeable and enlightened times. But if the introduction to this book taught us anything, it is that claims to truth are hard to make. As teachers, we have a responsibility to make sure that what we are teaching our students has claims to truth and honesty.

Our schooling system works by presenting students with knowledge, skills and understanding which has been neatly packaged into a series of subjects. This rather disparate group of subjects forms the structure and basis of the school curriculum. There are many voices in education who argue that subjects should not be the starting point for curriculum think-ing at all, arguing that they are the product of traditional curriculum thinking, constructs of a bygone era that simply sees students learning facts and taking exams to see how much they can remember. The mod-ern world is complex, information is readily available at the touch of a smart phone, and so young people need access to a different sort of curriculum.

What's it all about anyway?

Knowing why you want to be a teacher, or why you became a teacher in the first place, is an important starting point when we think about what we are teaching. Perhaps you have a passion for your subject and want to help the next generation to know the world through it; perhaps you see your role more as helping the young people in your charge to cultivate positive choices, behaviours and relationships. Maybe you really want them to understand the difference between assessment objective 1 and assessment objective 2. Either way, finding your passion is key if you want to sustain a career that could last for over forty years.

A lot of thought has already gone into defining the purpose of education. Educationalist Eleanor Rawling (2000) summarised a list of ideological traditions that influenced the activities in schools at the latter end of the twentieth century (Table 2.1).

Table 2.1: Ideological perspectives on the curriculum (from Rawling, 2000)

Ideological tradition	Characteristics
Utilitarian/ informational	Education primarily aimed at 'getting a job' and 'earning a living'. A focus on useful information and basic skills.
Cultural restorationism (as promoted by the New Right in English policy making in the 1980s and 1990s)	Restoring traditional areas of knowledge and skills (cultural heritage). Providing students with a set package of knowledge and skills which will enable them to fit well-defined places in society and the workplace.
Liberal humanist (also called classical humanist)	Worthwhile knowledge as a preparation for life; the passing on of a heritage from one generation to the next. Emphasis on rigour, big ideas and theories, and intellectual challenge.

Ideological tradition	Characteristics
Progressive educational (also called child-centred)	Focusing on self-development or bringing to maturity the individual student. Using academic subjects as the medium for developing skills, attitudes, values and learning styles that will then help them to become autonomous individuals.
Reconstructionist (also called radical)	Education as an agent for changing society, so an emphasis on encouraging students to challenge existing knowledge and approaches. Less interest in academic disciplines; more focus on issues and socially critical pedagogy.
Vocational or industrial trainer (Note: in some ways this cuts across all the other traditions)	Provides students with knowledge and skills required for work. Use workplace and work-related issues as a stimulus for learning skills/abilities. Use work-related issues for questioning the status quo.

Teaching through these different traditions creates wildly different school experiences. A curriculum that is progressive, or child-centred, will focus much more on the perceived needs of the child at the heart of the curriculum. A wholesome set of values and child-centred pedagogies, such as discovery learning, lead the teachers' thinking. Subject knowledge is less important, and perhaps even a distraction to the ultimate educational goals. In contrast, the cultural restorationist approach sees a more traditional, rigorous approach to education, with young people learning a defined set of knowledge – what could be called the 'canon' of academic knowledge. Here, pedagogy would focus on the learning and recitation of facts. A radical ideological perspective would see young people constantly challenging what they hear or read about, seeking alternative perspectives and challenging the orthodox position.

It is possible, of course, to think of a role for each of these ideologies. In the teaching of something like climate change, there will be times when learning knowledge to understand physical processes is key. At other times, you want students to respond to and empathise with people from across the world, and maybe even get them to think about radically different futures. Despite this, there is likely to be one or more of these ideological perspectives that resonates most when you think about why you became a teacher. Schools will too often promote a particular view of the curriculum, using that to drive their marketing and slogans. This may, or may not, align with your own values or, indeed, what actually goes on in the school on a day-to-day basis.

I have discussed Table 2.1 with a range of teachers, and at one conference it was proposed that there ought to be a whole new ideology added to the list: the 'exam outputs' ideology. Pedagogy would be teaching to the test and completing lots of practice papers. This suggestion was met with a lot of approval and seems to be the experience of many professionals. Perhaps we have lost sight of why we are teaching in the first place.

When it was first introduced into schools in England and Wales in 1988, the national curriculum had no overarching set of aims.[2] Instead, each subject was given a sort of mission statement. By the time ideological aims were added, the school system was already well established as recognisable subjects taught by expert specialists. The aims were tacked on later. In 2008, the three aims of the English national curriculum were to create 'successful learners, confident individuals and responsible citizens' (Qualifications and Curriculum Authority, 2008: 8). No talk of passing exams or learning any knowledge or gaining any skills. A decade later and these were scrapped in favour of a 'knowledge-rich' curriculum and a tighter focus on what children are actually learning (e.g. Department for Education and Gibb, 2021). For those of us interested in what we are teaching our kids this was a welcome refocus, but it seemed to ignore the need for students to develop skills and values, and perhaps took us away from developing character, confidence and responsibility.

In Scotland, the Curriculum for Excellence has as its aim four 'capacities' which help students become: 'successful learners', 'confident individuals', 'responsible citizens' and 'effective contributors' (Education Scotland, 2017). This is similar in aspiration to the curriculum of the early 2000s in England. The language of the curriculum in Wales is similar. Here 'four purposes' of the curriculum aim to create students who are:

● ambitious capable learners, ready to learn throughout their lives

2   Education in Wales became a matter for the Welsh government following devolution in 1999.

- enterprising, creative contributors, ready to play a full part in life and work

- ethical, informed citizens of Wales and the world

- healthy, confident individuals, ready to lead fulfilling lives as valued members of society

(Education Wales, 2020)

. . . .

The Northern Irish curriculum also has a language of key skills and broad 'areas of learning'. In each, there is no real mention of what students should be learning or why that might be considered important. Subjects are part of the learning experience, but they are a means to achieve these greater, child-centred goals.

Knowledge in the classroom: some starting points

To understand the sort of knowledge that teachers might engage with, it is worth dabbling into both philosophy and sociology. There are many different types of knowledge, as acknowledged by the ancient Greeks. Aristotle is often credited with inventing 'science' through his recognition of *epistêmê*, which was concerned with universal principles that can be uncovered, and *sophia*, which explains why things remain the way they are. Yet he also identified other types of knowledge: *technê* is knowing how to do something; *phronesis* is ethical judgement, using values and deliberation to work out actions in the world; and *nous* is about working out abstract principles and applying known ideas to unknown situations. Modern subjects draw, in part, from these ancient forms of knowing.

Epistemology is a branch of philosophy that focuses on how we know what we know, and how meaning is made. There are three epistemological traditions that can be of use to teachers: objectivism, constructivism and subjectivism. Each of the subject specialisms found in secondary schools will probably draw on one or more of these traditions when explaining to students how meaning and new knowledge is made.

Objectivism is the approach to knowledge that searches for absolute truths, separate from human intervention. Facts are facts. Their results can be replicated by different people at different places and times. Ideas such as the shape of the Earth or the answers to simple maths equations would be objectivist truths. The search for objectivist truth is at the heart of science and, as teachers of those subjects, we induct students into the ways in which we can reach these claims of truth.

Constructivism is where meaning is socially constructed by people. We derive meaning through interaction with an object or writing, which creates a shared understanding between the creator and the observer. Subjects which involve interpretation and recreation, such as English literature, often have a basis in constructionist thought. Teachers of these subjects help students to pick up nuance of language, tone, colour or stance, and to think about what this conveys to the audience. In turn, the students are able to create their own work, copying the style of others before developing their own.

Subjectivism is where a learner imposes their own meaning on the world. Creative subjects which require students to explore their own responses to phenomena, such as art or drama, could be said to be steeped in a subjectivist epistemology. Yet even this is not necessarily helpful. If students are responding to work that has been deliberately created to evoke a response, then this is more in the constructivist rather than subjectivist tradition.

Some of our subjects seem to fit well into these philosophies, and part of our role as teachers is to help our students to understand those traditions and how the subject 'works'. Yet these approaches are not able to categorise all school subjects so neatly. Geography, for example, encompasses knowledge created from different philosophical approaches. If a geography student is studying the physical processes in a river, then they are seeking objective truths, yet if they are studying the ways in which people inhabit and respond to the places where they live, then this is a much more constructivist epistemology.

Perhaps educational sociology might also help to offer some clarity for teachers who want to understand the nature of knowledge in the classroom. In *Social Realism, Knowledge and the Sociology of Education: Coalitions of the Mind*, Karl Maton and Rob Moore (2010) edit a collection of sociological approaches to the curriculum. As they describe, for many decades since the 1970s, sociologists were concerned with the 'false dichotomy' (Maton and Moore, 2010: 1) around knowledge; it was either completely objective and free from any human interference or it had to be socially constructed, created by someone for a specific purpose.

Objective knowledge was uncontroversial, and simply awaited human discovery. This has been described by Young and Muller (2010) as 'under-socialised' knowledge as people were absent from the process of knowledge creation. On the other hand, social constructivism identifies that all knowledge was created by humans and that varying claims to truths are made by different people. These could be scientists working on a new breakthrough or anyone posting information online – what Young and Muller (2010) call 'over-socialised' knowledge. This meant that it was difficult to make any claims of 'truth', as all claims were equally valid.

In a school curriculum, the knowledge taught to young people is what Michael Young identified as knowledge 'of the powerful' in his key 1971 text *Knowledge and Control: New Directions for the Sociology of Education*. This knowledge was created by people and organisations with the, perhaps unwitting, result of reinforcing power relationships, control and social norms in the classroom. Those who write the narrative can choose where our sympathies lie, and manipulate how we think about and respond to ideas. Much work has been done in educational sociology to identify those who create knowledge in schools and unpick the power relations that underpin this knowledge. Recent proponents of decolonising the curriculum highlight how the expansion of knowledge through the colonial experience, in all its forms, has contributed to our understanding and perception of the world and, therefore, how it is presented to young people in classrooms. Those who are actively researching decolonisation are seeking to find those hidden voices and experiences that have been lost along the way.

The result of much of this thinking in the 1970s and 1980s – much to Michael Young's frustration – was a mistrust of knowledge in the class-room and a rush to a more progressive style of curriculum thinking. If all knowledge is a human construction, then it is steeped in power relation-ships and therefore should not be the basis of modern schooling.

In response, in 2008 Michael Young wrote his seminal text, *Bringing Knowledge Back In*, in which he proposed moving from social constructiv-ism towards a social realist approach to curriculum thinking. Social realism acknowledges that knowledge is 'real' – having objectivity and replicability – but that it is 'social' in that it is created by people. Social realism identifies that some claims to knowledge are more valuable than others. Scientists working on a new vaccine can make greater claims to objective medical truths than a mystic healer can, for example. What makes their claims more valid is that they are from a group of experts, or *epistemic communities*, who follow a set of practices about how new knowledge is to be made, tested and verified. This is an ongoing process; new knowledge replaces old knowledge – it is never static. It is this that Young describes as 'powerful knowledge', an idea explored much further in the next chapter.

Under this approach to knowledge, it is possible to identify which claims to the truth have greater validity. For example, a team of biologists could work to create new knowledge in biological science by following the scientific method: identifying and then rigorously testing a new hypothesis, collecting and analysing data to draw conclusions, and putting their findings through a peer review process before publication. Their work then becomes part of the discourse of that disciplinary thinking and, as a result, has a valid claim to truth. Yet, even then, those findings can and should be challenged by other exerts in the same field who might propose a different theory.

Disciplined thinking in classrooms

Michael Young's work on social realism is focused on the school curriculum, but, of course, teachers in classrooms are not actively creating new knowledge. That is being done at universities by epistemic communities of experts in academic departments. These departments have disciplined ways of working, hence the idea of subject disciplines. The disciplined ways in which a mathematician thinks are different to the disciplined ways in which a historian thinks, yet each of these ways are more rigorous and scholarly than random musings in a blog post.

For secondary school teachers, part of our job is to help young people to understand our subjects' disciplinary thinking and the ways in which they create claims to truth – something explored across a range of subjects in Part II of this book. Some subject teachers, such as those teaching science, need to be more up to date with changes in the academic discipline as the rate of change is so quick; other disciplines, such as Classics, may change more slowly. Some specialists, of course, may reject altogether the idea that there is such a close relationship between the university discipline and the school subject. It is for this reason that teachers are expert subject specialists themselves. Or at least they should be. With teacher recruitment issues and a lack of funding, we often find ourselves teaching outside of our area of expertise.

Whilst it is easy enough to follow a textbook and teach a set of facts, helping young people to really understand how the discipline works is a greater challenge.

One of my favourite interview questions is: 'How do you know if someone is getting better in your subject?' The candidate's answer is always quite revealing about how they see their subject and how students gain and interact with knowledge within it. It could simply be that students are able to recall increasingly large numbers of facts, but I am always more interested in teachers who talk about students' ability to think like a scientist or a mathematician, and how that could be measured in some way.

One framework for thinking about the progression of knowledge, which teachers might find useful, is the idea of knowledge structures. This originates from the work of Basil Bernstein (2000). He identified two types of knowledge structure that are illustrated in Figure 2.1. In subjects that have a vertical knowledge structure, new knowledge relies and builds upon earlier knowledge. Mathematics could be used as an example here; students are unable to do algebra if they cannot multiply or divide. The knowledge of how to execute these functions is reliant, in turn, upon the ability to add and subtract, and, therefore, on being able to count and recognise number sequences. Over time, and through schooling, the mathematics that the students are learning gets increasingly more complex. This is why simply grabbing content from the university discipline and putting it in front of schoolchildren will not work, as they have not developed the conceptual building blocks on which that knowledge relies. Horizontal structures – the other knowledge structure that Bernstein talks about – are more common in the arts and humanities. Work covered in these subjects can be done in any order and does not rely on previous knowledge to be able to understand or access it. For example, if students are learning about Britain in the Middle Ages, there is no real need for them to have studied the Vikings or the Second World War first. Figure 2.1 illustrates this.

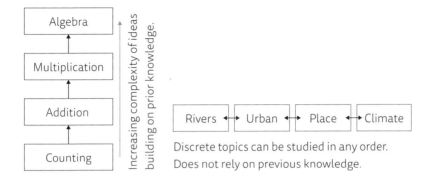

Figure 2.1: A visual representation of Bernstein's vertical and horizontal knowledge structures (from Bustin, 2019)

Like all good ideas in education these are not quite so straightforward. As we will see in Chapter 5, some writers (e.g. Rycroft-Smith, 2019) have questioned whether maths does in fact have a vertical knowledge structure at all. Even subjects with a horizontal knowledge structure rely on key strands of thinking that build and develop vertically. In religious education (RE), students might learn about the major world religions or ethics, and each does not rely on knowledge of another, but formulating arguments and considering and rebuffing counterarguments does take time to develop as a way of thinking. In geography, being able to use and interpret maps is something that is developed. The skills of a subject, being able to apply knowledge and understanding in a specific way, relies on deliberate practice over time. This has a vertical structure to it, even alongside knowledge that can be considered horizontally structured. Moreover, what students would learn in their studies of medieval Britain would be distinctly different depending on their age and stage, with increasing complexity and nuance of debate as they move up through the years.

Yet there is a further difficulty. As teachers, we cannot simply take ideas from the academic discipline and teach them to young people. The ideas are often highly complex and rely on a vast array of other knowledge, they are highly specialised or there are simply too many ideas to cover. Basil Bernstein (2000) talks of 'recontextualisation': the ways in which teachers take ideas from the academic discipline and make them accessible for young people in the classroom. Recontextualisation is a key work of teachers; it involves selecting what should and should not be included in a lesson, and the extent to which ideas are simplified and language modified. As a process, it can go wrong. Lessons can be over- or under-pitched in terms of complexity; misconceptions and misunderstandings can arise. It is easy for teachers to leave the work of recontextualisation to awarding authorities and textbook writers, who select and package content for young people, but it is rightly the work of teachers and part of our curriculum making (an idea discussed later).

What about skills and values?

It is easy to forget about skills in a chapter about different types of knowledge. Of course our students need to leave school with a range of skills! Much like the progressive vs traditional arguments, the knowledge vs skills debate rages on. A skill is the ability to do something. There are highly skilled sportspeople, highly skilled artists, highly skilled mathematicians. Yet skills and knowledge cannot be separated. A skill relies on knowledge; knowledge of how to do the skill; knowledge of what is happening. An example can be drawn from the world of golf. A skilful golfer will be able to putt a ball from a large distance, yet they will also need to be knowledgeable about the slope of the green, the wind speed and direction, the amount of force needed and the nature of the terrain. This knowledge may not have been taught by a teacher in a classroom, but it is there. It may well have developed through the golfer's self-reflection. A golfer with no knowledge of the game would not be very skilful. The type of knowledge needed to develop a skill can be described as 'procedural knowledge': knowledge of a procedure of some kind. With procedural knowledge, a person understands how to carry out a certain type of function that they can then practise to the point where it becomes a natural process, or, as some writers call it, an 'embodied' knowledge (e.g. Tanaka, 2011). In schools, some subjects have a much greater skills basis than others, with time spent practising a set of procedures. These subjects, such as maths and art, will have a large amount of procedural knowledge in their discourse, and teachers' time will be spent developing this knowledge to build these skills.

Schools also care about values: young people's ability to differentiate between right and wrong, to decide to follow a particular allegiance or to stand against injustice. Our education system would be lacking in any moral purpose if our students left school without caring for anything or anyone. Yet, much like the skills argument, the development of values requires the input of knowledge. Young people need to be exposed to different viewpoints, to hear arguments and counterarguments, to actively seek out different opinions. This can be challenging in an online environment that is filtering content without our knowledge. Michael Young's (1971) concern about 'knowledge of the powerful' is steeped in values discussions. The values young people develop could mirror those voices that have shaped the curriculum. In many of our subjects – particularly the humanities of history, geography and RE – these could well be steeped in colonial power relationships. John Morgan and David Lambert (2005) have called this type of teaching 'morally careless': teachers have not been careful enough to separate fact from opinion and rhetoric.

There is a further consideration to be made, and that is which – or whose – values we choose to inculcate and which we choose to challenge and unpick. This is where Tubb's (2003) ideas of 'public' and 'non-public' values can be of use. Our role as teachers is to let students see different non-public values and the knowledge that underpins them and come to their own considered opinion. Examples would include choosing a political affiliation and deciding whether to eat meat or buy fairtrade products, or not.

Values in the classroom can be a bit of a minefield for teachers to navigate, especially given cultural concerns, yet underpinning it all is knowledge. Knowledge becomes the building blocks of values and skills. Young people need to know how to do something (and why) in order to do it; they need to be able to know different sides of a complex issue before they consider their own response to it. Our role as teachers is to enable our students to develop this knowledge.

Types of classroom knowledge

There are many different types of knowledge that teachers help our students to grapple with in the classroom, and the nature of this depends on what subject we are teaching. The second part of this book explores the nature of knowledge in different school subjects, drawing on a set of knowledge classifications:

? **Core knowledge.** This is a set of concepts that forms the basis of a subject's curriculum. It has been labelled as the 'canon' of a subject; what needs to be learnt if someone is to be an expert in the subject. For subjects with a vertical knowledge structure, it might be easy to identify the core knowledge that young people will need at different stages of their education, but it is not so easy for those with a more horizontal structure. At best, it can help to provide a definitive base of subject content; at worst, it creates a tick-list of facts to learn.

? **Everyday knowledge.** This is the knowledge that students already have in their possession when they arrive in our classrooms. It is the sort of knowledge of the world that they will gain through experience, perhaps through their own reading or scrolling. As teachers, we can capitalise on this by starting to question them about what they already know. Everyday knowledge can be full of misconceptions. For example, everyone has heard of climate change, but our job as teachers, of course, is to move them beyond their everyday, surface-level knowledge.

? **Substantive (declarative or disciplinary) knowledge.** This type of knowledge is more ambitious than core knowledge. It is a way of expressing the knowledge make-up of subjects. It includes facts and processes, but also the ways in which subject knowledge is created and operates to create truths. This is why it has strong links to disciplinary knowledge: the disciplined thought processes needed to create claims to truth. Allied to this is the notion of indigenous knowledge, which can be defined as knowledge produced in specific socio-cultural contexts (Mistry, 2009). The extent to which this knowledge is transferable across contexts, or forms part of the main discourse, varies by subject.

? **Procedural (or non-declarative) knowledge.** This type of knowledge is know-how – knowing how to carry out a particular procedure that leads to or creates new knowledge. Having procedural knowledge can lead to the development of skills. In some subjects, knowing how to do something is more important than knowing a specific set of facts. Procedural knowledge thus becomes a more significant part of the way in which the subject works. If a particular skill, and the procedural knowledge on which it is based, becomes so well engrained that a person is able to do it almost without thinking, then this could be considered a form of embodied knowledge (e.g. Tanaka, 2011). This type of knowledge is often found in PE and creative arts subjects, as we will see later.

There are other ways in which to classify knowledge. Some writers talk about knowledges in the plural, arguing that there can be more than one way to reach truths. Another idea is that of a subject's gaze (e.g. in mathematics with the work of Paul Dowling (1998)): the ways in which people see the world from a subject's perspective. This would include elements of substantive and procedural knowledge. Powerful knowledge places the emphasis regarding what is being learnt on to the learner, focusing on how the knowledge becomes powerful for the individual. This is the focus of the next chapter.

Conclusions

So, what do we know? Knowledge is a complex idea. But we are knowledge workers and we must help our students to understand the world, the ways in which we make sense of it, and themselves. Subjects are not simply constructs from a bygone era; they have been around for centuries for a reason. They help to explain how the world works. Each subject does this in a different way, and that is why subject specialist teachers matter. Students don't study subjects in isolation. Students study a range of subjects, and this gives them a grounding in knowledge and truth. From their knowledge, students are able to develop skills and values to help them navigate the world.

For discussion

? Look at the list of ideological perspectives that underpin the curriculum. Is there one that you recognise as the way in which you see your role? Does your subject tend towards a particular ideology? Can you actively change and subvert that perspective?

? Can you identify the types of knowledge (based on the categories outlined here) that students engage with through your subject?

? Is there such a thing as identifiable core knowledge in your subject?

? What is the substantive and procedural knowledge in your subject?

? How do you know if someone is getting better in your subject?

Chapter 3

Whatever happened to powerful knowledge?

It was in a packed room in Harris Academy St John's Wood, London, on 8 September 2018 when powerful knowledge was elevated to the top of the government's education agenda. The event was a ResearchEd national education conference. The room was full of teachers and England's school standards minister, Nick Gibb, was delivering a speech. It was a wide-ranging take on the skills vs knowledge debate that has dominated education discourse, and his response to move us all on from these binary debates was to promote a curriculum built on powerful knowledge. Indeed, the term 'powerful knowledge' was used four times, as he argued in the speech: 'We must ensure that pupils are equipped with both powerful knowledge and the skills needed for this century' (Department for Education and Gibb, 2018).

Less than a month later, a *Guardian* article by Peter Wilby (2018) profiled Professor Michael Young, whose life work in educational sociology introduced the idea of powerful knowledge. This was a crowning moment for an educational concept that had only really begun life a decade before. Michael Young (2008) argued that we should be 'bringing knowledge back in' to educational discussions. Through many publications, including his own with David Lambert – *Knowledge and the Future School* (2014) – the concept was reiterated and refined. It was explored through curriculum development projects.[1] Papers were published, discussions and debates held, and the concept explored in depth.

What followed was an explosion of interest in powerful knowledge around the world. But then the inevitable happened. Like so many ideas before it, powerful knowledge fell victim to 'lethal mutations' – to use Jones and Wiliam's (2022) description – where ideas are taken out of

---

1   Including the one I was part of, GeoCapabilities 2, as well as my own doctoral research.

context, not really understood properly but discussed and spread anyway. The idea mutated in the hands of well-meaning but misinformed bloggers, social media users, school leaders and education writers until it became scarcely recognisable as what Michael Young had first written about. Suddenly, teachers were sticking the word 'powerful' in front of everything. You could download powerful worksheets and lists of powerful facts to learn for every subject. Use of the word 'powerful' somehow meant it was related to powerful knowledge.

In the same year as Nick Gibb's speech, Mary Bousted, the head of the National Education Union, the largest teaching union in the UK, argued: 'If a powerful knowledge curriculum means recreating the best that has been thought by dead, white men – then I'm not very interested in it' (as reported in Ward, 2018). Her thousands of followers lapped it up, reposted it and suddenly the concept became part of the battlefront of educational discourse, with Bousted using 'powerful knowledge' to wade into curriculum debates and position herself away from the political zeitgeist. The problem was that that is not what powerful knowledge means at all. By the time a few social media users, me included, politely pointed this out to her, it was too late. She did clarify her position in a later post on her Twitter (now X) feed, but the damage had been well and truly done.

Yet, even without its lethal mutations, there was already a large groundswell of criticism against the concept of powerful knowledge from a range of academic sources, both from those promoting other forms of curriculum thinking and from those who maintain that a curriculum built on knowledge (powerful or otherwise) is subject to inescapable power relations.

So, what is powerful knowledge?

Powerful knowledge is an expression of the ways in which subject knowledge can be truly empowering for young people. It is not a list of facts, nor a list of concepts, but an appreciation of the ways in which the specialised thinking that school subjects engender can enable students to think about the world in new ways. It takes students beyond their everyday knowledge. As such, it requires deep thought and rigorous engagement. It is knowledge born from the subject specialism, and debated by specialists working in universities who publish their findings in peer reviewed journals. Each of these different disciplines has their own unique claims to 'truth'. Powerful knowledge represents the best knowledge available in that subject at that time. But it is not static; it can be replaced at any time as new perspectives sharpen and new discoveries are made.

The challenge for teachers is in identifying what powerful knowledge is in practice. It could, potentially, include every discovery made in every subject discipline. Choices need to be made about what is taught in schools, yet this takes us back to the question of whose knowledge we are promoting and why. In response, what powerful knowledge asserts is that knowledge is constructed by people, but within epistemic communities of subject experts following the rules and norms of disciplinary thinking. Their claims to truth are 'better' and more rigorous as a result and, as such, could and should form part of a curriculum.

One of the implications of Michael Young's work is that teachers need to be subject specialists, and that they need to be given the freedom and trust to decide what to teach. Teachers are the experts, and recontextualise the knowledge from the academic discipline to make it available to students. There will be some difficult choices that teachers have to make about what to teach, and why, but that is their professional role. We need to trust teachers to make these decisions.

Back to the future

There is a broader framework of thinking about powerful knowledge which might be of use here. In their famous 2010 paper, 'Three educational scenarios for the future', Michael Young and his colleague Johan Muller identify three curriculum futures. These scenarios are not, in fact, some vision of what might happen but represent what is happening and what has already happened in schools. The three futures are called Future 1, Future 2 and Future 3 and have links not only to the knowledge vs skills debate that Nick Gibb was exploring in his now infamous speech, but also to the traditionalist vs progressive debate outlined in previous chapters.

These futures are explained in terms of what they might look like in a school, but in many ways they represent an attitude that teachers might take towards their work. Thus, the three futures heuristic represents ways of thinking about curricula as much as a tangible model of the school curriculum.

Future 1

The Future 1 curricular vision bears the hallmarks of the traditional, knowledge-rich curriculum. But knowledge in this vision is inert; it is a list of facts to be learnt and recited, akin to E. D. Hirsch's (1988) *Cultural Literacy*. The facts are not open to challenge and debate as they have been settled already; they are the core knowledge of the subject. A Future 1 curriculum sees the learning of facts as the end point. Students learn facts, derived from highly rigid school subjects that have strict boundaries. The more facts that are learnt, the more the student can be said to have achieved in the subject.

This approach to knowledge is exactly what Michael Young challenged in his discourse on 'knowledge of the powerful'. The core knowledge is 'set', but by whom and for what purpose? Textbooks are good at presenting facts and figures, but do not tell the story of how we came to know them. Under the Future 1 scenario, there are a series of curriculum gatekeepers who control and regulate what counts as knowledge, and what young people can and cannot know.

In Michael Young's discussions of what a Future 1 pedagogy might look like he cites the caricature of a nineteenth-century British private school, with schoolmasters in long gowns pacing up and down 'delivering' knowledge to their students, who are dutifully writing down what is said without question. Pedagogies associated with direct instruction tend towards Future 1 thinking. The didactic approach to pedagogy fits well with a Future 1 curriculum of compliance.

The Future 1 curriculum is highly critical of students gaining other skills and engaging with issues and values. It does not really allow young people to understand disciplinary thinking about how subject knowledge is gained. If we are serious about enabling our young people to be critical thinkers, then a Future 1 curriculum will not do.

Future 2

The Future 2 curriculum model is akin to the progressive vision explored in previous chapters. Subject knowledge is absent from the curriculum in any meaningful way, being replaced by a generic set of values, or vocational skills, at the heart of schools. It is akin to what Gert Biesta (2013) described as the 'learnification' of the curriculum; more emphasis is given to how the teaching occurs than to what is being taught. Subjects, if they exist at all, simply act as vehicles to enable these generic competencies to be developed. The Future 2 curriculum is developed out of a mistrust of the objectivity of knowledge. All knowledge is a human construct and, as such, all knowledge should be challenged and critiqued. For example, instead of a geography lesson on climate change aiming to help young people understand the complex processes of the greenhouse effect to explain the rise in global temperatures, it would aim to develop empathy or environmental concern. Thus, the scientific understanding takes second place to the development of an 'appropriate' emotional response. This has led to accusations of curricular 'corruption' (e.g. Whelan, 2007).

Future 2 pedagogies involve more student-led approaches, such as discovery learning, in which students are required to experiment and find things out for themselves without the help of a teacher. Teachers certainly don't need to be subject experts under a Future 2 approach. If the caricature of the Future 1 curriculum is a private school, then the image of a Future 2 curriculum is a progressive school in a deprived area where a vocational, skills-led curriculum is deemed more useful than one based on academic qualifications.

Future 3

Both Future 1 and Future 2 are deficient in many ways. Future 1 under-socialises knowledge; Future 2 over-socialises it (as Young and Muller (2010) describe). Knowledge is reduced to core facts to be learnt in Future 1 but omitted completely in Future 2. What the Future 3 curriculum tries to do is move beyond the simple binary. At the heart of a Future 3, social realist approach to curriculum is powerful knowledge, a term deliberately chosen by Michael Young as a play on his earlier phrase of knowledge 'of the powerful' (Young, 1971). This recognises that knowledge is significant in education, not in a way that involves learning facts but, instead, being inducted into a disciplined way of thinking. Students must engage with nuance and debate, scholarship and rigour as well as gaining the knowledge and understanding to engage with issues and develop skills. For Michael Young, the Future 3 curriculum, led as it is by powerful knowledge, provides a rationale for a subject-based contemporary curriculum. It provides a reason for employing subject specialists and supporting the development of their subject knowledge throughout their careers.

There is also a strong social justice element to Future 3. In Future 2, knowledge is deliberately undervalued in exchange for supposedly more valuable generic skills that would be of use in vocational careers. Yet in schools in more affluent areas, young people are traditionally fed a diet of knowledge which enables them to access university degrees and supposedly higher valued professions. Thus, there is an inequality embedded in the education system related to the attitude towards knowledge. Michael Young argues that all young people need to have access to powerful knowledge as a basic requirement of their schooling. It is only by enabling all students to be taught by subject specialists, under a Future 3 approach, that they have an equal chance to go on to the universities and professions of their choice. By deliberately offering them a different sort of curriculum, they will be unable to do this. So important is the social justice element of Young's work that the subheading to his and David Lambert's 2014 book is 'Curriculum and Social Justice'.

In their work on powerful knowledge in the history curriculum, Smith and Jackson (2021) further distinguish between traditional and radical social realism. As they argue:

. . . .

On the one hand we have a radical social realist position which aspires to social change through an emphasis on developing children's historical consciousness, while in the traditional social realist position the aspiration is that children who can think historically might succeed within society as currently constituted. (Smith and Jackson, 2021: 157)

. . . .

For them, the traditional social realist position is akin to Michael Young's thinking: access to high-quality history education will enable all young people to succeed educationally. However, for the radical social realists this is still not enough. Inequalities are entrenched at all levels of education, and no amount of good history teaching will change this without profound changes to what is being taught and why. Developing Future 3 curriculum thinking in schools is not about a didactic style of knowledge transmission, nor unstructured discovery learning based on play, but on careful pedagogical thinking. It is what Margaret Roberts (2023) calls 'powerful pedagogies'.

Powerful pedagogies

If a school wants to develop Future 3 curriculum thinking in practice, then there needs to be a consideration not only of what to teach but also how to teach it. In a stereotypical traditional Future 1 curriculum, in which knowledge is static, learning is by rote, copying out the textbook with little room for discussion. Future 2 sees a pedagogy that is unstructured; students learn by doing and by discovery but there is little guidance.

The sorts of pedagogies that support a Future 3 curriculum would be structured by the teacher to enable subject learning with student engagement. Margaret Roberts (2013: 204) argues: 'The use of enquiry-based approaches to learning can give students access to powerful ways of ... thinking, by helping students understand the nature of ... knowledge.'

Each lesson could have a question to drive the learning sequence. Students can then spend time engaging with different ways to answer that question, perhaps using some carefully selected source material (rather than giving the students free roam on the internet) before coming together to help answer the question. The teacher is key to this process, designing the enquiry, recontextualising knowledge from the academic discipline, selecting the materials for students to engage with and planning for progression in the lesson. This cannot be left to a non-specialist.

There are a range of activities that can help students to engage with subject knowledge, which can also teach them to think about their subjects. Although they will differ by subject, Table 3.1 shows some thinking skills activities that might be of use in a geography classroom.

Table 3.1: Some thinking skills activities for school geography lessons (from Bustin, 2017b: 142)

Thinking skills activity	Description	Example
Card sort classification activity	Information is provided on a series of cards, and students need to group them into categories, either their own or predetermined.	Categorising the impacts of overfishing as social, economic, political and environmental.

Thinking skills activity	Description	Example
Role play	Students take on stakeholder roles and debate an issue in character.	Planning issues enable students to take key player roles, such as local resident, councillor, and so on.
Odd one out	Students are given sets of four key words and have to work out which is the odd one out and why.	In a topic on settlement, four terms could be: city, conurbation, hamlet and urbanisation. Urbanisation would be the odd one out as it is a process; the others are types of settlement.
Taboo, Pictionary	Students have to get the rest of their team to say a key word by using their descriptions (Taboo) or drawings (Pictionary).	In Taboo, students would have to verbally describe the term river without using the words water, rain, flow or channel.
Living graph	Students are given statements and have to decide to which point on the graph the statement refers.	In a climate graph for a place, a statement could be: 'The rivers are in full flow and the temperatures are the lowest of the year.'
Mysteries	Students are presented with a problem and a range of clues to possible solutions. They read the information, maps, graphs and diagrams to solve the problem.	The enquiry question 'Why did Omar move house?' could have information on push and pull factors that students have to read about and unravel.

Thinking skills activity	Description	Example
Most likely to ...	This gets students to think about what conditions are likely in a given situation.	In a topic on urban geography, students could be asked which area of a city is most likely to contain the most litter, most pet cats, most foxes, and why.
Predicting with video	A video is played then stopped at a certain point, with students guessing what might take place next, before showing them what really happened.	Education videos can work, but better still are films and TV shows based on a geographical idea.

These examples are from a secondary geography teacher training handbook (Bustin, 2017b), but the ideas themselves derive from the Thinking Through series which was edited by educationist David Leat – for example, *Thinking Through Geography* (Leat, 1998), *Thinking Though History* (Fisher, 2000) and *Thinking Through Mathematics* (Wright and Taverner, 2009).

On their own, these thinking skills are not examples of 'powerful' pedagogy. When these books first appeared, they were readily taken up by teachers and became staple parts of teacher training in the late 2000s. The problem is that all too often the thinking skill itself became the most significant part of the lesson. The lesson objective became the completion of the activity. This is what Michael Young would consider Future 2 thinking. As a criticism of these types of publications in history education, Chris McGovern (2007: 76), in his contribution to *The Corruption of the Curriculum*, argues that they are: 'more concerned with leading immature youngsters towards superficial moral judgements than ... providing them with knowledge'. Skills and values are developed in isolation and knowledge is a distraction. In the rush to develop a knowledge-rich curriculum in the 2010s, many of these techniques were thrown out, considered part of the skills agenda that had no place in the knowledge-rich classroom. It was back to Future 1 thinking for all.

Yet this is an unfair legacy for these activities. In the introduction to his book, David Leat (1998) is very clear when he asserts that thinking skills activities are not ends in themselves, but a means through which students can gain subject knowledge. The end point is the subject knowledge; these activities are a way to 'think through' the subject. It is the discussion and feedback with students that is key to helping them develop powerful knowledge of their subjects. Thus, the lesson objective focuses on the learning of knowledge and the thinking skills activity becomes the route to get there. This again reinforces the idea that subject specialists are key in the classroom, as they are able to deploy activities to help students learn.

Powerful knowledge: the story of school geography

Whilst writers from a number of subject areas have explored powerful knowledge, geography has led the way. This is in part due to the work of Professor David Lambert, emeritus professor of geography education at the UCL Institute of Education. His book co-authored with Michael Young (2014), *Knowledge and the Future School*, developed the ideas further. Mark Enser's (2021) *Powerful Geography* explores powerful knowledge for geography teachers in a highly readable and accessible way. It is no surprise that shortly after publishing this landmark text, he went on to become Ofsted's chief geographer.

The exploration of geography as a powerful knowledge was explored through three funded curriculum research projects – GeoCapabilities 1, 2 and 3 – in the late 2000s through to the late 2010s. Education specialists and teams of geography teachers were asked to express how the powerful knowledge of school geography might be characterised. Alaric Maude (2016), an Australian geography educationist, identified five types of powerful knowledge. Type 1 is knowledge that provides students with 'new ways of thinking about the world' (Maude, 2016: 72). This would include the various concepts which underpin the subject, such as place and scale. Type 2 is knowledge that provides students with powerful ways to analyse, explain and understand the world. This would include the various processes that underpin the physical and human worlds. Type 3 is knowledge that gives students some power over their own knowledge. This includes being able to identify false claims to truth. Type 4 is knowledge that enables young people to follow and participate in debates of local, national and global significance. This includes clarifying the values inherent within complex issues and understanding the ways in which students can become active agents in the world. Finally, type 5 is broad knowledge of the world which takes students beyond their everyday understanding.

A further example of powerful geographical knowledge derives from the work of David Lambert and John Morgan (2010), here overlaid with Maude's (2016) types of powerful knowledge. Their three-stage expression of powerful geographical knowledge is shown in Figure 3.1.

Expressions of powerful geographical knowledge on which capabilities depend:

- *The acquisition of* deep descriptive and explanatory 'world knowledge'. This includes, for example, countries, capitals, rivers and mountains, also world wind patterns, distribution of population and energy sources. The precise constituents and range of this substantive knowledge are delineated locally, influenced by national and regional cultural contexts. **(TYPE 2)**

- *The development of* the **relational thinking** that underpins geographical thought. This includes place and space (and scale), plus environment and interdependence. This knowledge component is derived from the discipline. Thus, these 'meta-concepts' are complex, evolving and contested. **(TYPE 1, TYPE 3)**

- *A propensity to* apply the analysis of alternative social, economic and environmental **futures** to particular place contexts. This requires appropriate pedagogic approaches such as decision-making exercises. In addition to intellectual skills such as analysis and evaluation this also encourages speculation, imagination and argument. **(TYPE 4)**

Figure 3.1: An expression of the powerful knowledge of geography (Lambert, 2017, reprinted in Bustin, 2019: 122)

This work has tried to identify what is at the educational heart of school geography. It is not about defining core knowledge, as that would put us back in Future 1 thinking, where school geography becomes about learning facts. The first expression of powerful knowledge in Figure 3.1 identifies this descriptive element of the subject but stops short of defining it, arguing that it needs to be decided locally. This could be through a national curriculum of some sort or by geography teachers themselves deciding on the most appropriate content for their own students. This first point expresses the substantive knowledge of school geography – the places and processes underpinning the subject. It is what Maude (2016) describes as the analytical and explanatory concepts of the subject, and the ability to generalise complex ideas. The second expression of powerful knowledge is this idea of 'thinking geographically', linking ideas, processes, places and time to explain the changing world. Part of this is also about being able to uncover truth and think critically about the world. The final expression is concerned with the 'futures' element of the subject, with ideas about sustainability, choice and change over time. Maude's understanding of global issues at different scales is part of this third expression of powerful knowledge.

The ways in which these writers have expressed school geography are very different to the traditional split of the subject into physical and human geography that is often seen in schools. Physical geography takes a more scientific approach to explain phenomena such as rivers, coasts, weather and climate, whereas human geography draws from the humanities and social science to understand development, demography, people and places. Geography is determined by what you study, not how you study it. Hence, geography can be studied from a scientific perspective, following the rules of objective science, or in terms of how people look at and respond to locations, with meaning co-constructed between people and place.

These expressions of powerful knowledge attempt to draw the discipline together to identify the unique educational contribution that school geography makes. No other subject does these three things. Whilst other subjects, such as history, might mention places, these are simply a location for other events rather than an object of study in their own right.

The text below (from Bustin, 2017a: 100) shows a vignette that explores what this looks like in the school geography classroom, produced as part of the GeoCapabilities 2 project.

DESCRIPTION

My Year 10 class (15-year-olds) know that 'the Holderness coastline (on the east coast of England) is made from boulder clay'.

This is not everyday knowledge. But is it 'powerful knowledge'? I would argue that it is not, on its own, powerful knowledge. It is just a more or less correct 'fact'.

However, 'boulder clay' (or, more precisely, glacial till) could be conceptualised in a number of ways by different academic disciplines – chemists would be interested in its chemical composition, physicists might look at its tensile strength and the way it behaves under different stress and pressures. Geographers could look at it in a number of ways: for example, geomorphologists would develop their knowledge of boulder clay in terms of its physical properties of permeability, its tendency to slump and move under gravity and how it affects and is affected by its environmental context. To fully understand boulder clay geographically it needs to be placed within the context of its origins (from glacial deposition some 10–20,000 years ago) and its surroundings, which in the case of the clay on the Holderness coastline includes its location next to the sea. The actions of the sea (which can also be conceptualised in a number of ways) are of importance to understand the significance of the boulder clay as the wave action erodes the clay cliffs to cause rapid cliff retreat.

DISCUSSION

Our knowledge of 'boulder clay' (or glacial till) is shaped by the way it is conceptualised in the discipline of geography. For instance, we do not fully comprehend the significance of this phenomenon without knowledge of its origins, composition and location. It is this that makes it 'powerful'. It is almost the 'back story' of boulder clay – the way boulder clay is understood – that is indicative of the way geographers identify and describe it, and its significance.

The real value of this work is through envisioning what a Future 3 geography curriculum would look like in practice. When these three expressions of powerful knowledge are placed at the start of the curriculum planning process, it ensures that the result will have a strong knowledge component. From these, enquiry questions can be set to structure the courses and individual lesson activities to help students grapple with knowledge. Activities could include some of the thinking skills alluded to earlier, or more teacher demonstrations, or the more traditional approach of 'chalk and talk', but the key thing is that knowledge is the starting point of the planning, and the knowledge (and understanding) that the students gain becomes the end point.

Powerful knowledge: where did it all go wrong?

The concept of powerful knowledge has been written about extensively, and the fact that it infiltrated British education policy language shows how seriously it was taken. It has played a key role in influencing curriculum thinking in many schools, alongside other established educational ideas such as Carol Dweck's (2017) growth mindset, Rosenshine's principles of instruction (e.g. Sherrington, 2019) or Guy Claxton's (2018) work on learning power. Yet powerful knowledge has not become a central organising principle of all school curricula. This is due to a number of interesting factors, as well as critique, which those of us who take seriously the idea of powerful knowledge need to address.

Firstly, there is the politicisation of the idea. By being mentioned in a speech by a Conservative MP, powerful knowledge immediately became politicised; this was especially problematic as it was the Conservative government who forced the 'knowledge turn' in curricular thinking. This immediately alienated a number of teachers, despite social justice being a key tenet of Michael Young's ideas. All students need access to high-quality subject knowledge to give them access to the best possible futures.

There is also the problem of a lack of understanding of what powerful knowledge is, and our inability to express it succinctly. In an era when teachers are communicating via social media, the best ideas are the ones that can be explained in a single post. Powerful knowledge is not really like that and, as such, has been confused with knowledge of the powerful (such as the Mary Bousted example at the start of this chapter) or with learning lists of facts. Given that blog posts are not peer reviewed, many people wrote about powerful knowledge, or at least their version of it; some had read Young's work, but clearly a lot had not and that made the idea even less understandable. Much of the academic work around powerful knowledge is stuck behind pay walls.

Despite these two clear issues with communicating the concept of powerful knowledge, there are many legitimate critiques that have emerged over recent years. Professor Simon Catling, working in the field of primary geography education, questioned whether there should even be a hierarchical relationship between the university-based academic discipline and what goes on in schools. He wants young children to be able to explore their local surroundings in a meaningful way, and that does not rely on some meta-theory developed in a university. This is an idea returned to in Part II as it has implications for a range of subjects, such as PE and art, even at secondary level.

A further critique has emerged from some subject communities. For example, Robert Eaglestone (2021: 18), writing about English literature, argues that powerful knowledge is based around a scientific approach to understanding and, as such, scientism, 'the mission-creep of scientific ideas', has infiltrated the school curriculum. For him, English literature involves many values debates and discussions with students in which knowledge is co-created, which is antithetical to the idea of 'better' knowledge and a hierarchical relationship with a university discipline. This critique also applies to knowledge in the creative arts, as will be discussed further in Part II.

There is still an unanswered question over the 'power' of powerful knowledge. A number of writers have argued that the epistemic communities of disciplinary experts working in universities are themselves following sets of rules and norms that are steeped in power relations. Research only happens if there is funding for it, so rich organisations and funding bodies can ensure that certain fields receive a lot, whilst others are left out. Many of the rules of research are steeped in colonial traditions that perpetuate a Western hegemonic approach that ignores or trivialises folk traditions and indigenous knowledges. Studies into and from the Global South are dominated by voices and approaches from the Global North, and this is legitimised through publications.

Professor John White offers an even fiercer critique in a series of papers – such as 'The weakness of "powerful knowledge"' (2018) and 'The end of powerful knowledge?' (2019) – which provoked a response from other writers (e.g. Hordern, 2019). White questions the whole notion of power in the discussions and proposes the use of the term 'specialized' rather than 'powerful' knowledge. According to this idea, the starting point of curriculum thinking should be to identify what specialised knowledge(s) young people need in life and build the curriculum around this. It recognises the significance of knowledge but moves away from the rigidity of traditional subject boundaries. An example he uses is the climate crisis, which traditionally sits in both geography and science lessons but probably requires a specialised approach of its own. It also moves away from the overlying assumption that powerful is always good; not all specialised knowledge belongs on a school curriculum. As he argues of Latin:

. . . .

> Latin has its own kind of specialized knowledge [SK], but not every kind of SK merits a place in a compulsory curriculum and most would agree that Latin does not. (White, 2019: 437)

. . . .

The argument regarding the extent to which Latin can be considered a powerful knowledge is taken up in the second part of this book.

However, specialised – rather than powerful – knowledge still relies on people making decisions about what is and what is not taught in schools, but this time without the rigidity of subject specialisms. Cross-curricular teaching is not new, but it is done best when teachers are able to offer perspectives from their own subject specialisms. At the heart of powerful knowledge is the idea that it is never settled or static; there is always 'better' knowledge. It is a curriculum principle, born from the school subject experts rather than the university experts. If power lies anywhere, it is with the subject specialist teacher in the classroom. It gives agency back to the classroom teacher and celebrates (and trusts) their role as an expert. With a forward-thinking, Future 3 approach to knowledge, a teacher can listen to a variety of perspectives, new theories, arguments and ideas, and decide if this is better knowledge. The teacher in the classroom knows their subject and their students, and is best placed to make the decisions about what to teach and why.

Conclusions

The word 'power' has been used a lot in these discussions around knowledge. In many ways, this has proved to be unhelpful. Michael Young, when identifying the 'knowledge of the powerful', wanted to alert us all to the inherent, and often hidden, mechanisms of control over what was being taught in the classroom. By using the phrase 'powerful knowledge' he depersonalises the idea, making it about the knowledge itself, which has claims to being better and more rigorous than other knowledge. Another way for teachers to think about the powerful knowledge of subjects is to consider the ways in which knowledge is powerful for young people. This transfers the power onto the students themselves. It shines a light on what engaging with a particular subject will enable a young person to do, think or be. This is not about broad skills, as we would then be back to Future 2 thinking, and nor it is about what facts a young person can recite, which would take us back to Future 1. It is about what that young person will gain from studying that subject which they would not get from a different subject. In other words, how the knowledge studied in a particular subject is empowering for them in some way.

Discussions around knowledge that is empowering rather than powerful take us away from the distraction of power relationships in determining knowledge and recognises that young people themselves are able to gain knowledge, ideas, values, skills and attitudes through their education. They become empowered by the education they receive. It was this notion which framed much of the work of the GeoCapabilties 2 project. As part of it, Professor David Lambert asked geography teachers: 'In what ways is your subject a powerful knowledge for young people?' The answer to this question relies on teachers identifying what makes their subject unique in the curriculum – a difficult challenge in itself – but also thinking about why that knowledge is important. It is through these discussions that the idea of 'capabilities' emerges, and there is much more on this in the next chapter.

Part II of this book explores what this might mean for different subject communities. Groups of subject specialist teachers working in real schools were asked the same question: 'In what ways is your subject a powerful knowledge for young people?' They were also asked to illustrate it with a vignette of a classroom episode. Their responses to these questions provide the provocations for the chapters in Part II of this book. These answers matter, as knowing why their subject is uniquely important means they will remain focused on what they are teaching, and why.

For discussion

? How might the ideas of Future 1, Future 2 and Future 3 relate to the ideological perspectives on the curriculum explored in Chapter 2?

? Think about something you have recently taught. Whose knowledge was being presented? Where did it come from? Are there any alternate perspectives that might have been hidden from sight?

? Can you link Future 1 and Future 2 to particular political approaches to education policy, by both those in power and in opposition?

? How do you respond to these ideas and to the critiques of powerful knowledge? Is it a useful way to think about knowledge in the curriculum?

Chapter 4

Towards a capability approach to curriculum making

The Stockholm Concert Hall was lavishly decorated for the Nobel Prize award ceremony of 10 December 1998. Guests were dressed in their finery, the King of Sweden was in attendance to hand out the award and the stage was full of black-tie-wearing dignitaries. In his address, Professor Robert Erikson talked warmly about the achievements of that year's winner, the Indian economist Professor Amartya Sen. As he eulogised:

> You have applied a consistent approach in your studies of social choice, welfare measurement, and poverty. In theoretical and empirical work, you have deepened the understanding of these issues, making fundamental contributions to welfare economics. (Erikson, 1998)

A trumpet fanfare welcomed Sen to the front of the stage, where he shook hands with the king to rapturous applause from the assembled audience. A crowning achievement for a man whose life was dedicated to academic study and understanding social measures of poverty and welfare. Sen's Nobel Prize-winning work on the capability approach has been truly influential across a range of fields – increasingly, education and discussions about what makes a great education – and it is this application of his ideas that warrants inclusion in this book.

What is the capability approach?

Sen researched a range of interests across different fields. Yet it is his work on the capability approach in economics that is most celebrated internationally and most relevant to our discussion due to its educational applications. His 1980 lecture 'Equality of what?' started to challenge the orthodoxy of economic philosophy about what constitutes a 'good life'. This was developed through a number of works (e.g. 1985a, 1985b, 1987), including the book *Development as Freedom* (1999). He proposes that rather than measure the development of nations in economic terms, we should look instead at how free people are to live their lives in the way that they choose. As he argues:

> Development can be seen ... as a process of expanding the real freedoms that people enjoy. Focusing on human freedoms contrasts with the narrower views of development, such as ... growth of gross national product, or with the rise in personal incomes. (Sen, 1999: 1)

So, rather than quoting the gross domestic product (GDP) per capita of Saudi Arabia and Tanzania, and using those data to make comparisons about the countries, we instead look at the rights of citizens: the extent to which they have free speech, the ability to take part in democracy, women's rights, lesbian, gay, bisexual, transgender and queer (LGBTQ+) freedoms, etc. His work is about people, and the capabilities that these people have to make positive choices about how to live, how to be and how to do in a complex world.

It is a broad and ambitious philosophy which helped the United Nations to develop the Human Development Index (HDI), a composite measure of global development.[1] Using a range of complex equations, data on life expectancy, education (measured as mean years of schooling) and economic indicators (gross national income per capita) are combined to produce a numerical value somewhere between 0 (least developed) and 1 (most developed). Norway regularly tops the charts, and countries can increase in HDI value over time as quality of life improves or drop down the rankings if conditions in the country worsen.

---

1   See https://hdr.undp.org/data-center.

Whilst the capability approach focuses on what people are able to 'do', it is not completely divorced from economic measures of development. As a geography teacher, I often get my students to plot a scatter graph with GDP per capita (an economic measure) plotted against HDI. There is never a perfect line, and that can promote discussion and debate. Yet there is a broad correlation: the higher the GDP per capita, the higher the HDI. The more money a country has, the more they can invest in health-care – which will improve life expectancies – and education. The same would be true for a range of other social factors: the more wealth a country has, the higher its expenditure can be across a range of areas such as transport infrastructure and energy security (the ability of a country to meet its energy needs). Sen identifies this initial investment as 'commod-ities', but it is not a straightforward conversion from commodity to enhancing individual capability. He identifies capability 'deprivation' as a range of factors, from a political or social climate which prevents, for example, women travelling alone or an LGBTQ+ person acknowledging their relationship in public. These deprivations prevent a person from being truly free.

Individual or community capabilities enable choices about how to 'func-tion' in life (these are terms that Sen uses in his framework). This can be utilitarian in nature, choosing to follow passions or desires, or it can be about having agency to make a positive difference. What is important, however, is that people are able to make deliberate choices. He cites many illustrative examples, but a key one is experiencing hunger. A per-son could live in a country which is experiencing famine, or a person could choose to fast as part of their religion. The key difference is that there is an element of personal choice and agency in the latter example, which means they have more freedom to follow a life of their choosing.

What has frustrated many supporters of Sen's ideas is that he never iden-tified what capabilities might actually look like in practice. The HDI, which developed from his work, chose to focus on life expectancy and education. In this chapter, I have identified things like women's and LGBTQ+ rights, but these are not drawn specifically from Sen's writings. He is deliberately vague when writing about individual choices as differ-ent people will have different priorities. Thus, for Sen, each society can define and review what their capabilities might be.

As a means to build on Sen's capability approach, a range of other writers have begun to list and define what they consider to be universal capabili-ties (and these are usefully summarised in Alkire, 2002). The US philosopher Martha Nussbaum (2000) has been particularly influential here in creating her list of universal capabilities. She identified a set of 10 basic capabilities: life; bodily health; bodily integrity; senses, imagination and thought; emotions; practical reason; affiliation; other species; play; and control over one's environment ((a) political and (b) material).

For Nussbaum, these are basic capabilities that are needed by all, giving people the freedom to choose how to live a life that they find fulfilling and desirable. Other writers' lists bear some similarity, with bodily health, integrity and wellbeing being central. Interaction between Sen and Nussbaum showed her frustration that Sen was never able to endorse her (or anyone else's) list of capabilities, and Sen's resolute refusal to do so is discussed in a range of publications (e.g. Nussbaum, 1988; Sen, 2004). Nussbaum's list has been critiqued as offering a white, North American, middle-class view of the world, lacking in any empirical basis (e.g. Stewart, 2001). This would seem to chime with Sen's view that defining capabilities should be left to local situations, so that people are able to decide on the most appropriate set for themselves, their families and communities.

Back to school: the capability approach to curriculum thinking

The broad framework of thought that Sen devised has been readily taken up by educationists who are interested in the success of education systems. In the same way that Sen argued that is it too crude to measure a country's development in purely economic terms (such as GDP), so too we could argue that the success of an education system is not simply in measurable outputs like exam data, pass rates or the percentage of students achieving A*–C grades. Instead, in line with the capability approach, we should look at how the education system affords young people the capabilities to live a fulfilling life; to have freedom to particate in society and in the democratic process; to make positive choices about how to live in the modern, complex world.

Framed like this, the capability approach can be used to express the values and purposes of education, and Melanie Walker and Elaine Unterhalter's (2007) edited book, *Amartya Sen's Capability Approach and Social Justice in Education*, explores this notion. What is striking is that both this work and Michael Young's *Bringing Knowledge Back In* (2008) have social justice as a key thread running through their arguments. For

Young, access to the powerful knowledge of subjects should be a right of all young people, irrespective of background, and for Walker and Unterhalter, the capability approach can be used to list capabilities that all young people need to be able to achieve through schooling, also irrespective of their background.

Through Walker and Unterhalter's work, and others on the topic (e.g. Bustin, 2019), Figure 4.1 shows how the capability approach could be conceptualised in educational discourse.

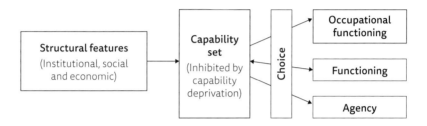

Figure 4.1: The application of the capability approach to education (from Bustin, 2019: 112)

Much like work on the capability approach to development, the individual is at the heart of this model. In this instance it is the student themselves at the core. The student, through their education, develops a capability set. This itself is the product of a range of structural features, such as the nature of the institution and its values, and the nature of the curriculum; social features, such as the nature of the young people themselves; and economic features, such as how much money has been spent on resources and the learning environment.

It is capabilities that enable the young person to make choices once they have finished their schooling. These would include occupational choices – or 'functionings', to use Sen's term – about what to do to earn an income and what career to pursue, and more generic choices regarding how to live and individual agency: being an active and engaged citizen, being politically active and making positive life choices.

In the same way that Sen never identified a set list of capabilities, this conceptual model does not identify what educational capabilities are. It is not, however, about qualifications or the measurable outputs of education. This model is concerned with how education can help young people to develop personal abilities rather than the ability to pass exams.

Table 4.1 shows two lists of suggested capabilities from Lorella Terzi (2005) and Melanie Walker (2006).

Table 4.1: Educational capabilities

Terzi (2005)	Walker (2006)
Literacy: Being able to read and to write, to use language and discursive reasoning functionings.	**Practical reason:** Being able to make well-reasoned choices.
Numeracy: Being able to count, to measure, to solve mathematical questions and to use logical reasoning functionings.	**Emotional resilience:** Being able to navigate study, work and life.
Sociality and participation: Being able to establish positive relationships with others and to participate without shame.	**Knowledge and imagination:** Being able to gain knowledge of a chosen subject – disciplinary and/or professional, its form of academic enquiry and standards. Being able to use critical thinking and imagination to comprehend the perspectives of multiple others and to form impartial judgements.
Learning dispositions: Being able to concentrate, to pursue interests, to accomplish tasks and to enquire.	**Learning dispositions:** Being able to have curiosity and a desire for learning.
Physical activities: Being able to exercise and being able to engage in sports activities.	**Social relations and social networks:** Being able to participate in a group for learning, working with others to solve problems and tasks.
Science and technology: Being able to understand natural phenomena, being knowledgeable on technology and being able to use technological tools.	**Respect, dignity and recognition:** Being able to have respect for oneself and for and from others.
Practical reason: Being able to relate means and ends and being able to critically reflect on one's and others' actions.	**Emotional integrity and emotions:** Not being subject to anxiety or fear which diminishes learning.
	Bodily integrity: Safety and freedom from all forms of physical and verbal harassment.

Terzi's list is generated from her work with students with special educational needs and, as such, could be seen as a minimum curricular entitlement for all students. Walker's list is derived from her work in higher education. Translated into school curriculum thinking, both identify the role that acquiring knowledge plays in helping students to develop capabilities. For Terzi this is through literacy, numeracy, science and technology, and for Walker this is encapsulated by 'knowledge and imagination', which includes knowledge of a chosen subject. Yet subject knowledge is not about being able to recite content but rather is a form of enquiry; it is about learning how to think within the subject. This bears similarities to the way in which Michael Young talks about knowledge, seeing it as a disciplined way of thinking, not as a set of facts to learn. The rest of the capabilities in both lists are more generic competencies and learning behaviours.

But what about knowledge?

Much of the early discourse on the capability approach to education can be critiqued regarding the role that knowledge, skills and values play in this process. Indeed, if you search for 'capabilities' and 'curriculum' online, what is returned is a series of links about generic teaching resources that are akin to Future 2 thinking. Qualifications and measurable outputs are inherent in the model; a young person who has achieved a set of high grades will have more choices open to them, particularly in terms of occupational functioning. Yet, if knowledge can be built into this model, its usefulness as a curriculum principle improves. A young person studies a range of subjects and engages with the different types of knowledge of those subjects. This then gives them a capability set, derived from all the subjects they have studied. Each person's capability set will differ as the students have studied a range of different subjects, but their capability set can enable a young person to make positive choices, to be empowered in life.

To further this idea, Geoff Hinchliffe's (2006) work looked at what capabilities might derive from studying humanities subjects (geography, history, philosophy and sociology) in higher education. His list of capabilities is:

- Critical examination and judgement.
- Narrative imagination.

- Recognition/concern for others (citizenship in a globalised world).

- Reflective learning (ability to articulate and revise personal aims).

- Practical judgement (in relatively complex situations).

- Take responsibility for others.

(Hinchliffe, 2006: 12)

This list takes us closer to understanding why the humanities subjects might have intrinsic value, yet on closer inspection what seems to be missing here is any reference to the sorts of knowledge(s) that humanities students might engage with. The ideas around taking responsibility and being reflective are worthy in themselves but not directly the outcomes of a humanities education. Students who study art or drama might well consider these to be outcomes of their education too. What is needed, then, is a more rigorous approach to subject knowledge and how that might contribute to capabilities. By combining Michael Young's (2008) work on powerful knowledge and the capability approach (Sen, 1980; Nussbaum, 2000) to education, a curriculum conception arises which reveals important ways in which we can consider the aims of education and the role of knowledge.

Within a school, students study a range of subjects, each taught by a subject specialist. The students engage with the powerful knowledge of the subject – the substantive knowledge of concepts, processes and facts, and the procedural knowledge of how to think within the subject – as well as develop a range of subject-specific skills. In turn, this helps the students to develop a range of subject-specific capabilities, and a capability set derived from their whole educational experience. It is this capability set that is really empowering. It gives young people choices about how to live; how to be, to act and to do; how to make choices about work (or not), consumption, travel, causes and acting on beliefs. What an educational capability set might be like is explored in the conclusion of this book.

This is ambitious curriculum thinking. It really opens up the educational potential of school subjects beyond passing exams (hence the title of my 2019 book: *Geography Education's Potential and the Capability Approach*). It is at the heart of the capability approach to curriculum and could be a manifestation of Future 3 curriculum thinking.

It seems a long way away from where a number of schools are currently, with a near obsession placed on examination results and teaching to the test. Then there are those schools where the more generic skills and values agenda has corrupted the curriculum so much that knowledge is seen as irrelevant. Or those where classes are taught by non-specialists, where students might well learn the facts needed to pass a test, but the real grounding in the thought processes of the subject is underdeveloped.

If each subject is able to contribute in a meaningful way to a young person's education, then the obvious next question is to consider what the powerful knowledge of each subject might be that can enable capabilities, and how subjects all work together towards a broader set of educational goals. The second part of this book begins these conversations. Much of this thinking has already happened in geography education, in the discourse on GeoCapabilities

Back to the story of school geography: GeoCapabilities

At the time of writing, there have been three internationally funded curriculum research projects which have explored the role that geography as a school subject (the 'geo') plays as part of a broader capabilities curriculum. The GeoCapabilities projects explored the unique contribution of geography to a young person's education, using Michael Young's framework of ideas around powerful knowledge as the language to express it. The full story of GeoCapabilities is told in a range of publications both academic (e.g. Lambert et al., 2015; Bustin, 2019) and for teachers (e.g. Young and Lambert, 2014; Enser, 2021).

Figure 4.2 was developed as part of the exploration of school geographical knowledge and how it contributes to a broader capability set.

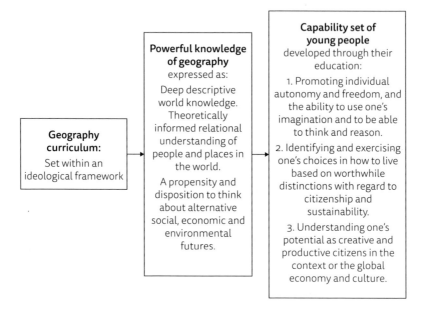

Figure 4.2: The connection between the school geography curriculum, powerful knowledge and capabilities (based on Solem et al., 2013, from Bustin, 2017a: 135)

In this example, the capability set draws on Nussbaum's work on human capabilities. The powerful knowledge of geography is based on an early iteration of David Lambert and John Morgan's (2010) work. Powerful knowledge becomes the bridge which connects the school geography curriculum to the development of human capabilities. The implication is that geography needs to be a central part of every student's educational experience. Without it, a young person will miss out on significant parts of their education.

Back to the classroom: the making of a Future 3 curriculum

The ideas explored in this chapter can be made relevant for teachers through curriculum making. A key proposition throughout this book is that teachers need to be in the driving seat of the curriculum; not waiting to be told what to teach by senior leaders, textbook authors or exam boards but actively thinking about what they want to teach and why. Teachers are the curriculum makers in a Future 3 curriculum.

Curriculum making explores the ways in which teachers, students and subject knowledge interact. It goes beyond individual lesson planning but occurs at a more conceptual level. One way to illustrate this is through the model shown in Figure 4.3. Different versions of this model have appeared in a number of publications (e.g. Lambert and Morgan, 2010) and this one has been readily shared in the geography education world.

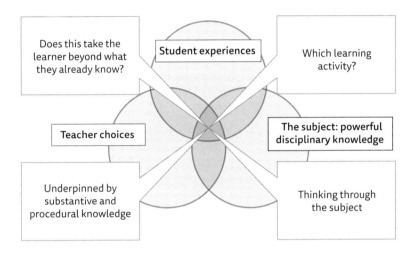

Figure 4.3: Curriculum making in schools (based on Lambert and Morgan, 2010)

According to this model, three considerations need to be kept in balance in a curriculum (shown by the three overlapping circles). The first is the subject itself, expressed here as powerful disciplinary knowledge, with 'disciplinary' identifying the important role that the university discourse plays in informing the school subject. The second is student experiences. Students come to our classes with everyday knowledge. Some students may have studied what we are about to teach them before; others might have seen a social media post about it and think that they are an expert. Bringing the subject and the students together are teacher choices – choices about what to recontextualise from the vast disciplinary knowledge available and why, and choices about how to teach the material, both in terms of pedagogical approaches and the needs of the students. A lesson at the end of the day on a Friday afternoon might look very different to the same lesson with the same class on a Monday morning, and these decisions might inform what is being taught when and why. The four speech bubbles emerging from the centre of the diagram illustrate some of the thought processes that teachers need to have in mind. Everything is underpinned by the knowledge (substantive and procedural) of the subject, and the ways in which thinking can be developed within the subject. The choice of learning activity will help to take students beyond their everyday knowledge into something new.

The dominance of any one of these three areas leads to an imbalanced curriculum. Too much emphasis on student experiences and we are back to Future 2 thinking; too much focus on subject knowledge and that is Future 1. At the heart of this diagram, where all three areas interact, is where Future 3 thinking becomes possible.

The conceptual interaction of subjects, students and teachers that this model shows is not unique to the UK. The German, French and Nordic tradition of curriculum 'Didaktic/didactic'[2] refers to these three ideas, modelled as a triangle, as shown in Figure 4.4.

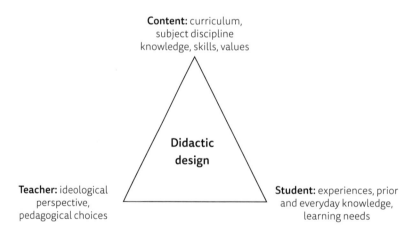

Figure 4.4: The didactic triangle (adapted from Smith, 2012)

---

2   Part of the reason why the didactic triangle has not really infiltrated UK education discourse is probably due to the word 'didactic'. In UK discourse, didactic teaching refers to teachers reading or speaking aloud and students writing down what is being said verbatim. Whilst this style of pedagogy has a place in teaching (for example, it can be very good for specific definitions or the spelling of difficult words), the meaning of the term is more limited. In the UK, at least, curriculum making has become the bigger idea.

This model contains the three curriculum making elements – content (knowledge, skills and values), the students and the teacher – but around that is a series of further considerations. Assessment and evaluation appear as part of the wider model, as do instruction, tools and pedagogy, which refers to the ways in which the content is taught.

The ambitions of a Future 3 curriculum are holistic, knowledge driven and futures orientated. As such they show a real similarity to another European educational concept of 'Bildung', which has been defined by the Global Bildung Network (2021) as follows:

> Bildung is the combination of the education and knowledge necessary to thrive in one's society, and the moral and emotional maturity to be both a team player and have personal autonomy … Bildung is knowing one's roots and being able to imagine and co-create the future.

Knowledge is at the heart of Bildung; however, the concern is not just with academic knowledge but everyday knowledge, folk traditions, and religious and moral aspects of student life.

Conclusions

The capability approach can be seen as another articulation of the grand picture of the school curriculum that was explored in earlier chapters, alongside various ideological perspectives. What sets this apart is the idea that teachers and school leaders are very much in control of thinking about, deciding on and creating what capabilities look like in practice. Sen always maintained the idea that capabilities will differ from society to society, and the educational equivalent is that each school is able to shape capabilities in the way they choose, as will be returned to in the conclusion. To build capabilities as part of a Future 3 curriculum, we must focus on what knowledge is needed, and this leads us back to discussions around types of subject knowledge.

Many of the arguments drawn in this chapter and the previous two were developed by experts and researchers in school geography. Their translatability across other school subjects has been more piecemeal, so the second part of this book explores what an ambitious, Future 3, capabilities curriculum might mean in different subject disciplines.

For discussion

❓ Have a look back at the lists of educational capabilities proposed by Terzi and Walker. How relevant are these for your school? Would you add or change anything?

❓ How might your subject contribute to the educational capabilities discussed in this chapter?

❓ Think about your next few lessons with a particular class. How might the curriculum making model be a useful approach to planning these lessons?

Part II: Theory into Practice

Introduction to Part II

The ideas explored in the first part of this book present an ambitious view of the school curriculum. By interacting with the powerful knowledge of our subjects, taught by subject specialist teachers, young people will be able to develop capabilities that will mean they can leave school and go on to live lives they truly value. It invites teachers to rise above exam-focused day-to-day school life to really allow subjects to shine, and to think about what we are teaching and why.

Yet the chapters in Part I are theoretical. They could easily have been written by people who have not seen the inside of a classroom for many years – in fact, for many of the writers cited that is indeed the case! It is easy to read the theory and think it wouldn't work in my school or for my subject. This part of the book explores that notion in more detail.

The impetus for Part II of the book is inspired in part by Gericke et al. (2018: 441), who acknowledge a lack of research into powerful knowledge across the whole curriculum – in their case in the Swedish school system – asking, 'How can the nature of powerful knowledge in different school subjects be characterised?' This book now offers some original research to help address that question.

Teacher voice

To add some authenticity to the discussions that follow, a small-scale research exercise was set up involving teachers from three separate secondary schools. This was done as part of their regular cycle of professional development. The exercise took the form of a lecture and workshop delivered over half a day, following a similar format:

? All teachers in the school took part and were asked to sit in their department teams.

? The first part of the session involved an introductory lecture about many of the ideas explored in the first half of this book: the concept of curriculum and why thinking about it matters, powerful knowledge and the importance of subject expertise.

? After the lecture, teachers had to discuss the following question: 'How, and in what ways, does your subject offer young people the powerful knowledge on which their future capability will depend?' To help, the example of school geography, as presented in this book, was given to them to use as a structure.

? In the final part of the session, a representative from each department fed back to the rest of their colleagues. They had to succinctly express what the powerful knowledge of their subject might be. This was collected as a written contribution and the findings appear in this part of the book.

The first of these workshops took place as part of the dissemination phase of the GeoCapabilities 2 project (as reported in Lambert et al., 2015). The initial lecture was delivered by Professor David Lambert, who had a leading role in the project. The second workshop took place to see if there was a difference in the thoughts of teachers from a second school; it was only designed to confirm any findings. What I discovered, as you will see in the subsequent chapters, is that there is often a discrepancy between teachers in different schools regarding what makes their subject a powerful knowledge. The third school, then, was introduced as a way of triangulating the findings. Each workshop was independent, and teachers did not get to see the previous teachers' answers.

The final session took place completely online due to restrictions in place during the COVID-19 pandemic. As such, teachers from this school were asked to type their contributions, and to create an illustrative vignette similar to the example from school geography. This is a short description of a classroom episode in which the teachers explore something they have taught to a particular class, unpicking it to think about exactly what was being taught. This was an opportunity to illustrate how classroom teaching might link to the wider aims of their subject curriculum.

The three schools have been anonymised throughout this book. During the workshops, teachers were told that any data they create might be published and discussed in some way. The small-scale research was unfunded (except for the first workshop which was completed as part of the GeoCapabilities 2 project) and undertaken by me as a lone researcher following ethical guidelines from the British Educational Research Association (2018). Outcomes from the first two schools were briefly presented in my previous book (Bustin, 2019), with limited discussion. This section builds on that introduction. In all, over 250 teacher voices have fed into the pages that follow.

Limitations of the research and how the data are used

It is important not to overstate the role of the research featured in this book. Although 250 voices is a large number, three schools is not. If time and funding allowed, then repeating this study for a larger number of schools across the country, and possibly world, would increase the validity.

As a result, the data from the teachers feeds into the discussion rather than leads it. There are instances, as you will see, where there is a fair degree of commonality in what the teachers from the three schools are saying about the nature of knowledge in their subjects. There are times when they focus on different things, but no attempt is made to try to explain that based on the nature of their schools – there is just not enough evidence to support any claims like that. There are times when the responses do not seem to link to the task. There could be a range of explanations for this, including genuine misunderstanding, but the responses are taken as they were produced. In at least one workshop, I noticed, anecdotally, one teacher using his phone to try to look up a 'correct' answer. Make of that what you will!

There were some challenges on the day which may have affected the nature of the responses. Some teachers are not specialists, in the sense that they are teaching a subject in which they have no formal qualification. This makes the task of really exploring the nature of the subject more challenging. Some teachers taught in more than one department, and so were asked to join the one they taught in most of the time. The response is a collective one, but the extent to which the task was delegated to the newest teacher or tackled by the head of department alone is unknown.

What the teachers say about knowledge in their own subjects is used as a provocation for each chapter. Based on their words and the literature, a response to the research question ('How, and in what ways, does your subject offer young people the powerful knowledge on which their future capability will depend?') is provided to try to express the ways in which their subjects can be considered a powerful knowledge for young people.

Conclusions

What follows is a series of chapters, each focusing on a different area of the school curriculum: mathematics (Chapter 5), English literature and language (Chapter 6), science (Chapter 7), humanities (Chapter 8), creative arts (Chapter 9), languages (Chapter 10) and physical education (Chapter 11). There is no set structure to each chapter as they do not each conform to the same blueprint; there are often arguments that warrant discussion in one subject which may not appear in other subjects. Generally, however, the first part of each chapter explores what the literature says about the nature of knowledge in that subject and starts to explore what powerful knowledge might look like and whether it is a useful framework. The next part of the chapter presents the outcomes from the small-scale research. Finally, a response is provided about whether and how the subject could be considered a powerful knowledge for young people.

It is envisaged that not every chapter in Part II will be read by everyone. If you teach, or are training to teach, a particular subject then it would make sense to go straight to the relevant chapter. If you are responsible for the whole-school curriculum, then all the chapters may be of value.

Chapter 5

What might make mathematics a powerful knowledge?

There was a book published in the mid-1960s which challenged the established ways in which mathematics was being taught. It purported to offer a radical new alternative to the methods used in the Western world. The book, *Vedic Mathematics*, by Indian monk Bharati Krishna Tirtha was published posthumously and based on his life's work and teachings. His methods are reportedly based on mathematical techniques developed during the Vedic period, a time of classical Indian pre-history (c.1500–c.500 BCE). The techniques were supposedly translated from ancient Sanskrit texts. There is a romance associated with ancient wisdom and, given their classical links, the teachings became popular. Vedic maths is on the syllabus in a number of Indian states and is popular with Hindu nationalists. You can find the techniques in a range of subsequent publications and online teaching materials.

Critics have argued that, despite the book's claims, there is no evidence that any of the mathematics were developed in the Vedic period. The original texts that the techniques supposedly derive from were never produced as supporting evidence. The book contains a series of quick tricks to help with mental arithmetic, which can be of use to students, but some have argued that these actually take longer to calculate than conventional mathematics. Vedic maths has not been taken up widely, but the story of its teachings remains a fascinating insight into the ways in which new mathematical knowledge can be claimed.

Mathematics knowledge

Mathematics is a central subject in education systems throughout the world. As a subject, it is a science of numbers and patterns in 'pure' or conceptual form, or 'applied' into other disciplines, such as engineering, physics or statistics. In her book on curriculum, Ruth Ashbee (2021: 67) explains, 'We find ourselves in a universe where the physical realm behaves in mathematical ways, and where mathematics can be applied to yield many descriptive, predictive, and material gains.'

The Arabic numeral system (0,[1] 1, 2, 3, 4, 5, 6, 7, 8 and 9) has become globally dominant, although other systems do exist and have over time. Roman numerals (I, II, III, IV, V, VI, VII, VIII, IX, X, and so forth) are included in the English school curriculum. All students study mathematics from the start of compulsory school through to age 16. Maths is one of the two compulsory GCSE subjects that students must pass in order to access further education and the widest range of employment opportunities.

Knowledge in mathematics takes many forms. Cosette Crisan (2021: 241), in her chapter on mathematics in *What Should Schools Teach?*, explains how new maths knowledge is derived through 'manipulating ... abstractions through deductive reasoning [which] often results in the identification of new relationships, leading to the discovery of new knowledge and/or to testing for the validity of new ideas and/or to the discovery of "truths"'. Ruth Ashbee (2021: 67) observes, 'new knowledge is made in mathematics in the postulations, developments, and proofs of conjectures and in developing new techniques and applications'. Thus, maths is less a distinct 'body of academic knowledge' that needs to be passed on, but more a knowledge of how to explore systematic problems according to a set of distinctive mathematical rules.

According to Basil Bernstein's (2000) knowledge structures, mathematics is often cited as a classic example of a subject with a strong degree of verticality: students can only progress further once more basic foundations of knowledge are laid. Students need to know how to count before they can do arithmetic; arithmetic needs to be mastered before algebra. There is a natural inbuilt hierarchical knowledge, and school mathematics follows this broadly, although teachers still have considerable choice over the order in which to teach certain topics. This makes mathematical

---

1   Zero is an interesting mathematical idea. It was not introduced in the numbering system we know until around the eleventh century (according to https://www.history.com/news/who-invented-the-zero). Notice that there is no Roman numeral for zero.

knowledge similar to scientific knowledge. Yet other writers have argued that this is not the case at all. Dr Cathy Smith suggests that maths is more like sociology, with different specialised 'languages' like probability and algebra; however, 'one language doesn't displace or disprove the other' (quoted in Rycroft-Smith, 2019: 1). She argues that therefore there is a strong degree of horizontality to mathematics knowledge.

A crude way of looking at one key evolution in mathematics as a discipline is the change from a practical knowledge designed to solve real-world problems, such as calculating areas of land, through to a knowledge that was more intrinsically valuable. This is mathematics for the beauty of working on, engaging with – and not just solving – abstract problems. The ancient Greek mathematicians saw a beauty in patterns that was not directly related to solving a problem in front of them. Examples such as Pythagoras' theorem are still central to the modern maths curriculum. Mathematics is not just about finding the right solution but understanding the method through which that answer is derived. The balance between getting to the right answer and understanding and enjoying the process that led to it is a central contention at the heart of school mathematics.

School mathematical knowledge

Epistemologically, one way to approach mathematics is as a method for searching for objective truths inherent within phenomena. School maths is not about learning a set body of mathematical rules to get to 'an answer' but to 'think mathematically'. According to the national curriculum for England (Department for Education, 2021), the aims of mathematics are for students to become 'fluent in the fundamentals of mathematics, including through varied and frequent practice with increasingly complex problems over time, so that pupils develop conceptual understanding'. Ashbee (2021: 67) sees similar aspirations for school mathematics, arguing that 'students of mathematics are brought into unique ways of seeing ... To see the behaviour of mathematics and to live-in it is to see rational, elegant truth in the world, and it is beautiful.'

The substantive knowledge of school mathematics would be the key facts and principles that underlie the subject. This would include a list of the various topics being studied, such as algebra or quadratic equations. In her book *Curriculum: Theory, Culture and the Subject Specialisms*, Ashbee

(2021) presents a diagrammatic version of school mathematical knowledge in which she identifies broad areas of knowledge: of ratio and proportion, number, geometry, probability and statistics. Alongside this runs knowledge of algebra, which informs all these other areas.

The procedural knowledge of mathematics would include the various ways in which mathematical problems can be explored and solved. This is often how the subject is conceived in schools, and this overfocus on problem solving has led Brian Hudson (2018: 386) to argue that 'an overemphasis on practice, presents a fragmented view of the subject and reduces standard procedures simply to rule following'. The ubiquitous use of a calculator makes this task even simpler and reduces opportunities for deeper thought. The overemphasis on teaching to the test and creating a need to get to the right answer has created a school subject that focuses too heavily on developing the procedural and substantive knowledge of mathematics – the different topics and rules to follow – rather than helping students to gain more of the knowledge that helps them to think mathematically (Hudson et al., 2015). This creates a mathematics curriculum forged in Future 1 thinking. As Crisan (2021: 245) explains:

nowadays, for most learners in secondary schools in the United Kingdom geometry is mainly about 'shape and space' without reason, deduction or proof, the focus instead being on calculations of lengths, perimeters, areas and volumes ... School children need opportunities to engage with proofs and the abstract. Proof is a fundamental component of the discipline of mathematics and so it should be part of mathematical education in schools.

In research with primary school teachers, Hudson et al. (2015) identified that the framing of the school maths curriculum stifled students' creativity and limited their autonomous problem solving. The school system values measurable outputs, and this creates a mathematics curriculum in which:

the excessive pressure from high stakes external testing and inspection, and the associated heavy emphasis on drill and practice, can establish circumstances that ... lead learners of mathematics to experience it as something to be feared and as anxiety inducing, boring, demotivating and alienating from the subject itself. (Hudson, 2018: 389)

Thus, Hudson fears that a focus on drilling correct methods for solving problems can be alienating for young people and will not nurture their love of mathematics. In his book *What Your Year 6 Child Needs to Know: Fundamentals of a Good Year 6 Education*, E. D. Hirsch (2014) explains what good school mathematics looks like for 10- and 11-year-old children. Much like his famed *Cultural Literacy* (1988), the book contains a set of quite specific maths facts that children should know. For example, when explaining what children should know about comparing integers, Hirsch (2014: 215) identifies the specifics: 'In general remember the following rules: (1) a positive integer is always greater than a negative integer and (2) the farther to the left a negative integer is from zero, the less its value is (-1>-100).' In his critique of Hirsch's work, Hudson (2018: 392) argues:

> First, there is a very strong emphasis placed on practice, second, a disconnected and fragmented view of the subject is presented, and third, there is a tendency towards rule following and to reducing standard procedures simply to rule following.

This approach can result in a low-quality mathematics education, rooted in Future 1 thinking, with the aim that teachers identify who can 'do' maths by following a set of predetermined rules. In her book on maths education, *The Elephant in the Classroom: Helping Children Learn and Love Maths*, Jo Boaler (2009: 2) explains why this attitude towards the subject is wrong:

> In many maths classrooms a very narrow subject is taught to children [which] involves copying methods that teachers demonstrate and reproducing them ... But this narrow subject is not mathematics, it is a strange mutated version of the subject ... When the real mathematics is taught instead – the whole subject that involves problem solving, creating ideas and representations, exploring puzzles, discussing methods and many different ways of working – then many more people are successful.

A far more ambitious approach to school mathematics, which Boaler would promote, is one in which an understanding of the procedural knowledge is also part of the learning. It is what Hudson (2018) refers to as 'knowing that' and results in a deeper understanding of how we arrive at the answers. Crisan (2021) discusses how this type of knowledge is known as 'syntactic knowledge' within the maths education discourse. It encompasses the way in which the rules, the nature of enquiry and new knowledge is introduced and accepted. Alongside the list of substantive topic areas, Ashbee (2021: 68) also highlights the importance of developing 'habits of working mathematically', and what Paul Dowling (1998: 33) calls the 'mathematical gaze'. This is a way of seeing the world, as Dowling (1998: 6) explains, 'as if the mathematician casts a knowing gaze upon the non-mathematical world and describes it in mathematical terms.' This is a broad and ambitious way of thinking about school mathematics. It is in understanding this that the 'beauty' of the subject (as Ashbee so eloquently describes) can be revealed. This is also a possible reflection of the powerful knowledge of mathematics and the capabilities that come from this.

What makes mathematics a powerful knowledge for young people?

Two purposes emerge from the literature about the value of a mathematics education. The first is a broadly utilitarian one – it is useful to know maths so a young person can work out how much things will cost in the shops, or what they will pay back if they take out a loan, or their chances of winning if they play the lottery. The second is the intrinsic value in learning how to think mathematically and seeing beauty in numbers and logic.

Mary Myatt (2018: 185) discusses what a maths 'mastery' curriculum might entail, and how powerful mathematical knowledge might be expressed. She suggests that there are three elements to this:

1. The principle of fluency (number bonds, times tables, place value) – these need to be learnt and secured, and built up slowly over time. This would take the form of the substantive knowledge of maths – the 'know how' identified earlier.

2. Reasoning. Getting students to think about what they are about to do rather than rushing straight in to find the right answer. Students could come up with alternative methods to reach the same answer.

3. Problem solving – this is where fluency and reasoning 'come to life'. (Myatt, 2018: 185)

. . . .

For her, these three elements mean that 'pupils can talk about what they are doing, the other possibilities for working out an answer and why some might be more efficient or appropriate in a particular context' (Myatt, 2018: 184). To encourage teachers to do this sort of curriculum thinking, Myatt draws on the work of Karen Wilding who asks students questions such as: 'What do we notice?', 'What do you expect to come up with, roughly?', 'What makes you think that?' (quoted in Myatt, 2018: 184). Answers to these questions could develop students' mathematical reasoning. Although not part of her three-stage approach, Myatt adds a fourth idea: understanding where mathematical knowledge has come from and the struggles to understand what we now know. I suggested that powerful knowledge is in part the backstory of a fact – how it arose and what people thought before. There seems little opportunity to include this type of material in the current curricular conception of school mathematics.

Engagement with mathematical thinking can be an expression of the powerful knowledge of mathematics. This would help to develop students' mathematical capabilities, encouraging them to think about the world in new ways, to go beyond their everyday experiences and to interact in and with the world.

Teacher voice

Table 5.1: Results of mathematics teacher workshop

School A	School B	School C
This subject is the study of concepts such as quantity (numbers), structure, space, and change. These concepts allow us to model real-world situations and facilitate understanding thereof. This also enables us to predict outcomes of future events. The knowledge and application of skills to problem solving in general. The abstraction of skills to other disciplines.	Ability to solve problems (the beauty of maths is not in solving the specific problem but in developing the skills to problem solve). Learning to see the world differently. Learning to learn. Training different parts of the brain. Resilience. Cross curricular links to other subjects is where powerful knowledge is developed.	Developing a framework to approach solving problems, not only in maths but in the wider world. Learning that making mistakes isn't a bad thing but part of the process of reaching an end goal. Numeracy is important for individuals to develop logical thinking and reasoning strategies in their everyday activities. We need numeracy to solve problems and make sense of numbers, time, patterns and shapes for activities like cooking, reading receipts, reading instructions, finance and even playing sport. To develop the critical thinking and analytical skills required to flourish in a data-driven world.

The mathematics departments in all three schools were amongst the biggest, as maths is compulsory up to the age of 16 and each school had large numbers of students choosing to continue with mathematics at A level. School A contained two non-specialist maths teachers whose ideas were included in the research.

The teachers in the three schools all seem to have different conceptions of how the powerful knowledge of mathematics might be expressed. School A starts with a broad attempt at listing some of the substantive knowledge of the subject; this was not included at all in School B's response. The notion of problem solving appears in both lists, but in School A this is not about specific maths problems but using maths to solve problems 'in general'. Much of what School B identifies as mathematics powerful knowledge is in fact more generic, holistic skills akin to the Future 2 thinking – learning to learn, brain training, resilience, and more. Whilst a good mathematics education will likely enhance all of these generic competencies, they are not unique to mathematics (other subjects can claim they help children to develop resilience).

Both schools A and B pick up on the extent to which mathematics links to other subject disciplines. As it is a core subject, much curriculum time is devoted to mathematics, and in part this is due to its utility across other school subjects. Science subjects rely on numerical data presentation and manipulation, and these techniques are introduced in mathematics before being applied to other subjects. Yet this gives us a further challenge. If we are relying on other subjects to express the unique educational contribution (expressed here as capabilities) of mathematics, then we can hardly claim that mathematics has anything original to contribute to an educated person.

The contention identified in the literature about the balance between doing maths to get to an answer and doing maths to develop mathematical thinking (a term not used by the teachers in the case study schools) is not evident in the way School A reflects on its powerful knowledge. The first point the teachers in School B identify – 'the beauty of maths is not in solving the specific problem but in developing the skills to problem solve' – is similar to Mary Myatt's discussion of the maths in her mastery curriculum. The use of the word 'beauty' is significant, too, as it suggests there is something much more significant about solving maths problems than simply getting to answers, akin to notions of developing a mathematical 'gaze' (e.g. Dowling, 1998).

The team of teachers in School C was asked to illustrate their curriculum thinking in the form of a vignette:

. . . .

In Year 9 statistics we teach students (13- to 14-year-olds) how to calculate averages and ranges from a data sample. On the face of it this knowledge is a set of simple instructions that yield a numerical result. It is, however, understanding the way in which this data was collected and the results used that transforms this into powerful knowledge. At GCSE we talk a little about what a sample is, but at A level we look more closely at different sampling methods to avoid bias and ensure proper representation of a given population. Getting students to think about correct representation unlocks the idea that the statistics they see in real life could come from a carefully selected sample to give the desired outcome. This understanding is crucial to those going on to any social science related degrees where theories and hypotheses are tested using samples. Within this unit of work they start to look at how they could choose or represent data to support a particular argument. This leads on to how data can be misleading and misrepresented in the media. At A level we look at how claims are tested to a certain degree of accuracy and how sample size affects this. Students learn to question the statistics and diagrams thrown at them by governments and adverts and look for the small print of how many people were sampled and to what degree of accuracy. Like many methods in maths, working out an average is relatively simple and something which most people can do. Understanding the process of how it is obtained and how it can be manipulated is what makes this topic 'deeper knowledge'.

. . . .

The ways in which these teachers are reflecting on their curriculum is very different to the ways in which Hirsch (2014) presents the mathematics curriculum in terms of specific testable facts to learn. The teachers here have focused on one area of substantive knowledge, the teaching of statistics, to one year group, Year 9 (13- to 14-year-olds). Rather than trying to identify a list of what students need to know, which would be Future 1 thinking, they have explained that it is 'understanding the way in which this data was collected and the results used that transforms this into powerful knowledge.' It is this focus on the procedural knowledge that gives the subject its emancipatory power to get students thinking. Their vignette also explores more deeply the connections between mathematics and other subjects, fulfilling the subject's role as a 'core' curricular component. Here, they have cited social science degrees and the use of statistics within their discourse but not made links to other school subjects.

Another element of the powerful knowledge of mathematics that emerges in the vignette is the role that the subject can play in addressing some of the key challenges of fake news, media bias and online filter bubbles. As the teachers here identify, students 'start to look at how they could choose or represent data to support a particular argument'. The understanding of this gets more sophisticated at A level, with a look at sample sizes and degrees of accuracy. Thus, through mathematics the knowledge needed to verify factual claims and to develop a critical response to data is enhanced.

Based on the literature, and the voice of the teachers presented here, the powerful knowledge of mathematics could be expressed as follows:

❓ Knowledge of the rules of mathematics to solve numeracy problems. This includes an increasing complexity from addition through algebra to statistics.

❓ Being able to identify solutions to mathematical problems and finding alternative solutions to the same problem. Identifying problems and ways to express them mathematically. This has often been called 'thinking mathematically'.

❓ Knowledge of data manipulation: presentation, claims to representativeness, relative bias and reliability.

❓ Knowledge of mathematical problems of the past and how they have been solved in the real world.

❓ Knowledge of how mathematics can aid understanding in other data-reliant subjects, especially the sciences.

Conclusions: towards mathematics capabilities

The powerful knowledge of mathematics can be expressed in many ways. Its substantive knowledge includes a range of different topics. These can be seen as being broadly hierarchical, which gives the curriculum content a natural progression from early years (counting, number bonds) through primary school and into senior years of study. Each of these areas have 'rules' that need to be learnt and regularly practised for mastery; it is through this that mathematical accuracy can be enhanced. The more complex and sophisticated the rules for solving equations become, the more creative and flexible the student needs to be to solve them.

Yet there is much more to mathematics. The powerful knowledge of mathematics can also be expressed through thinking mathematically and developing a mathematical gaze – understanding why answers are obtained in a particular problem and seeking alternative methods to reach the same outcome. This is what transforms mathematics education from simply solving equations to understanding mathematics. Powerful knowledge can be expressed through an understanding of where data comes from and how reliable that data can be to make claims about truth. This will enable students to understand the extent to which presented truths can be reliable and declared with statistical certainty. Powerful knowledge of mathematics could also be expressed through students gaining a deeper understanding of the development of the discipline itself. This could be done by presenting ancient real-world problems to modern students and seeing if they can work out how the problem was solved. A classic example here would be the challenge that Eratosthenes faced when trying to calculate the circumference of the Earth (as described in Chapter 1).

Together, these enhance students' capability to think about the world in new ways, to be rigorous and methodical, to be attentive to detail, to solve problems logically in different ways, and to be actively engaged with claims of truth and validity.

For discussion

? Research Vedic maths techniques. Do these have a place in the modern classroom?

? How can you impart the 'beauty' of mathematics to students?

? Is mathematical knowledge more horizontally or vertically structured, according to Bernstein's classifications?

? How important is it to link maths in the classroom to maths in the real world, and, if it is, how might this be achieved?

? Should students be allowed to use calculators or other digital technologies in the classroom?

? If other subjects rely on students' understanding of mathematics, how could you support your colleagues who teach these subjects in delivering content coherently?

? If a class of students are approaching problems using different techniques, but arriving at the same solution, is this problematic?

Chapter 6

What might make English literature and language a powerful knowledge?

English literature is the subject that introduces students to some of the greatest writing humanity has created. Top of the list of great writers in the English language is surely William Shakespeare; a national survey conducted by BBC Radio 4 for the turning of the year 2000 voted him the 'British Person of the Millenium' (*BBC News*, 1999). He wrote at least 37 plays and 154 sonnets, many of which have gone on to inspire generations of playwrights, writers and actors. His works have been published and translated the world over and films have been made of his plays and even of his life. His works are readily studied in the English classroom, whether it is younger students getting lost in the fairy world of *A Midsummer Night's Dream* or older students engaging with *Hamlet* or the love story of *Romeo and Juliet*. There are believed to be only about 235 copies of the First Folio – a compiled collection of his work put together shortly after his death. In 2020, one sold at auction for £7.6 million (*BBC News*, 2020).

Shakespeare lived from 1564 to 1616, but his life is shrouded in mystery; there is not much evidence beyond a few key recorded dates and a few personal documents. As a result of this lack of historical data, a number of scholars over hundreds of years have questioned whether Shakespeare is indeed the true author of the works attributed to him. In his famous work of 1920, '*Shakespeare' Identified*, J. T. Looney proposes that the works were created by Edward de Vere, the seventeenth Earl of Oxford. De Vere was a skilled lawyer, articulate and bright, and had travelled to many of the places that feature in the plays. He would also have been familiar with the workings of the royal court, something of which an actor from Stratford-upon-Avon (as Shakespeare was) would have had limited experience. Part of the reason de Vere kept his anonymity, so the story goes, is that he did not want to be associated with such a lowly profession as writing, and nor did he want to put his name to plays that were overtly political. Thus, he chose to write under a pseudonym, picking a local actor to put a face and a name to his famous works. There is a slight problem with this theory, which is that Edward de Vere died in 1604 and some of the greatest plays, such as *King Lear* and *Macbeth*, were published after that date. This problem was addressed rather imaginatively in the 2011 film *Anonymous*, which told the story of de Vere, Shakespeare and the greatest works of the English language.

For many, this debate matters greatly; for others, it is a fun distraction. Yet one of the recurring questions about interpreting works of literature, as we shall see, is the extent to which the context of the writing is key to understanding it. Knowing the socio-cultural backdrop to the events in the work or knowing something about the writer might help students to make sense of it. Clearly, if the identity of the writer somehow changes then the interpretations, and what the work means, could be altered.

English in the curriculum

English is a core subject in the national curriculum in England, compulsory from the start of school through to age 16. Along with mathematics, students must pass their English GCSE examination to progress to the next stage of their education. In primary schools, there is a focus on literacy and learning to read and write, and the level of sophistication in the texts increases as the children get older. The rules of English language are introduced as students go through school, grammar and spelling being two key components. The fluency of writing becomes the focus, as this is a key ability across a range of other subjects, such as history, where arguments need to be constructed and defended. The examination system sees students writing answers using pen and paper in almost all subjects. It is for this reason that English is seen as a core and essential subject.

The focus on writing, as well as the push towards a knowledge-led curriculum over the last decade, has led to an overfocus on easily assessable elements of the subject. As Professor Michael Hand (2021: 17) has pointed out, 'Well-intentioned teachers, responding to the demands of their senior management teams, try to teach English as if it were chemistry.' Chemistry, as a science, has a distinct vertical knowledge structure, where new knowledge relies on previous knowledge, and this gives the school subject an architecture that allows easy assessment at different levels. A focus on examination outputs has seen revision guides telling students how they should be reacting to set texts, following prescriptive pro formas for essays, and all of this reduces the subject to a series of easily achievable goals. Yet English does not function like that; there are elements to English proficiency that cannot be captured as formulaic writing responses. Mary Myatt (2018: 165) is keen to offer a broader approach to English beyond just writing. As she argues:

I want to make the case that the speaking, listening and reading elements [of an English curriculum] should have higher priority. The reason I believe they don't have a higher profile is because the 'gains' are not immediately visible in the way that writing is.

Her argument is that writing is easy to assess and, as such, has become a key part of schooling, whereas more attention should be given to oracy, listening and reading.

Literacy and language have become two key tenets of the school English curriculum; indeed, at GCSE, students are required to sit separate exam-inations on each aspect of the subject. Yet they are unequal. In her chapter on English literature in *What Should Schools Teach?*, Alka Sehgal Cuthbert (2021: 60), who is also one of the editors of the book, argues:

As language came to be more closely associated with literacy, and literacy levels with social mobility, attention to literature fell by the wayside. The legacy of these developments continues to inform curricular English today.

She observes that there has been more focus on basic literacy and, as such, time and energy spent on literature has reduced. Yet the division between literature and language has been called a 'distraction' (Ashbee, 2021), as they each rely on the other to aid understanding.

Knowledge in English

The substantive knowledge of the subject would include literary traditions, as well as the knowledge required to make sense of specific texts. This might mean looking at knowledge in other subjects, such as history, if that knowledge is key to enabling access to a particular text. The procedural knowledge of English would be the various rules of grammar, punctuation and spelling, which help with written articulation of ideas. It would also include the knowledge required to make sense of a text, such as the rules of textual analysis and poetry interpretation.

As a student reacts to and interacts with a piece of literature they are constructing meaning, derived as much from the text as from their response to it. This suggests that knowledge is co-constructed, with the student playing a role in making meaning. It is their interpretation of the text, guided by a teacher and in discussion with other students, that creates the meaning. Eaglestone (2021: 12) goes a step further, arguing that discussion with others is key to making meaning in English:

> You can't do English by yourself ... knowledge is made by all the people in the classroom together as they develop their own 'ideas and emotions' and do not simply recall things deposited or drilled into them. The experience of being moved (or left stony-hearted or bored) by a story is part of the educative process in English.

Students co-constructing meaning through interaction with each other and a text is not an automatic process, however; a teacher is key. The teacher's role is to pick the text, guide discussion and teach any substantive knowledge that the students might need (such as socio-historical settings or key allusions which need further explanation). The teacher also gives students the procedural knowledge needed to make sense of a text – how to do it – which should guide the discussions.

Given this bold claim about how knowledge is generated it seems antithetical that the examination system requires students to see a text for the first time and make sense of it on their own under exam conditions. Here there is no room for dialogue. The high-stakes examination system sees students tested on a set of pre-selected books and poetry that have been taught in lessons. Yet there is a further problem here. Given the high-stakes nature of assessment, revision guides exist on all sorts of texts which students can read, memorise and discuss in an exam. They tell students what they should be thinking or feeling about a text. Poor teaching can, of course, do the same thing; students are told what to think rather than how. As Eaglestone (2021: 16) explains:

the worst tradition of 'assessment-itis', is simply trying to drill students, parrot-fashion, with what they should think, feel and say about a work of literature, which betrays both the discipline and the point of literature. Indeed, forcing students to mimic beliefs they do not hold and that do not correspond to their experience is the best way to put them off literature altogether.

Ruth Ashbee (2021: 98) has further unpicked the types of knowledge that students are able to engage with in the English classroom. As she argues, 'of all the human cultural pursuits, literature, above all others, deals with the human condition ... literature covers everything in the Self'. English helps students to understand themselves and each other in a way that other subjects cannot.

As part of understanding the human condition and the self, a challenge in English literature is the extent to which the background and context of the writer should feed into student understanding. There is disagreement within the discourse, and Wimsatt and Beardsley's celebrated 1946 article argues that it should not. As they state, 'the design or intention of the author is neither available nor desirable as a standard for judging the success of a work of literary art' (Wimsatt and Beardsley, 1946: 468). Students read the text and, through discussion with each other and a teacher, use the evidence from the text to create meaning and understanding. The text is able to stand alone, devoid of its time and place of origin, allowing young people to reflect on the words within their own context and understanding. The conditions in which the writer wrote the text are either in the text itself or irrelevant.

Yet for Hirsch (1967), the writer created the text for a purpose, and knowing this is central to devising meaning. A writer's background, location, time and place will inform their writing, and if 'the meaning of the text is not the author's, then no interpretation can correspond to the meaning of the text' (Hirsch, 1967: 5, emphasis in the original). This idea suggests that text does in fact have a set meaning, awaiting discovery by students, and, as such, there are correct and incorrect interpretations of texts.

Seeing the subject in this way makes setting examinations and assessing progress much easier.

One area in which students are empowered through the study of litera-ture is in the development of values. Rather than these emerging naturally as an outcome of a good English education, Eaglestone (2021) sees engagement with a range of values as implicit to understanding texts in the first place. As he argues:

. . . .

Values are how we orient our discussions of literature ... Without understanding that Satan is evil – a value judgement – *Paradise Lost* makes no sense. The study of literature is where we discuss, com-pare and discover our values: it is *value-rich*. (Eaglestone, 2021: 16–17, emphasis in the original)

. . . .

This moves values discussions beyond simple clarification or transmission and into an integral role in the ways in which knowledge is co-constructed. Additionally, it is for this reason that Eaglestone disagrees with Young's (2008) idea of powerful knowledge being applicable to English, as powerful knowledge is meant to be 'value-free'. Engagement with values therefore requires the skilled and careful role of the teacher. An English teacher needs to be able to help students navigate values effectively. This relies on knowledge.

Ruth Ashbee (2021) identifies a range of types of knowledge that help students to engage with and through texts. These include, in summary, knowledge of ways of looking – for example, metaphor, story, argument, pattern; knowledge of the theory of texts (fiction, poetry, plays, transac-tional writing and other non-fiction) – for example, knowledge of themes, genre, rhetoric, argument, structure, meter, alongside other ideas; knowl-edge of contextual knowledge – for example, history, geography, politics, the human condition, and so on; knowledge of words – their meaning, connotations, morphology and etymology; and knowledge of grammar – for example, knowledge of word classes, syntax, tenses, and so forth. All of these feed into, and are fed by, reading well – for example, habits of reading text and checking for meaning, intentionally drawing inferences where they are not obvious, habits of internal dialogue about meaning, characters, claims, and more – and writing well – for example, knowledge of types of sentence, techniques and use of language, knowledge of plan-ning and redrafting, etc.

Despite this comprehensive articulation of the types of knowledge in English, she offers a warning:

attempts to compartmentalise or itemise knowledge in English carry the danger of leading to damaging, reductive effects because they can miss or distort the intrinsic anarchy of knowledge in the subject. (Ashbee, 2021: 98–99)

These discussions have looked at the ways in which students gain knowledge through the shared reading of texts, but one debate in English education is about which texts to teach, and why. It is during this discussion that accusations of curriculum corruption are levied.

English literature as a corrupt curriculum

English literature as a school subject has come under intense criticism over the choices of key texts studied as part of examination courses. As a subject, it is very much on the front line of ideological debate between those who see the canon as something to be protected and valued and those who argue that these works perpetuate social norms and inculcate a white, Western view of the world that suppresses more diverse voices. As Sehgal Cuthbert (2021: 54) explains, 'literature has become hostage in a culture war where one side sees little good in what is new and the other sees little good in the past'.

In the introductory chapter of this book, I quoted Michele Ledda's (2007: 18) comments in *The Corruption of the Curriculum*, in which she argued that Carol Ann Duffy is on the curriculum at both GCSE and A level, 'not because she is a greater poet than Milton, but because she is more "relevant", dealing as she does with very contemporary issues such as disaffected learners'. These criticisms have far-reaching consequences for teachers of English. Sehgal Cuthbert (2021) cites an article in *The Telegraph* (Turner and Somerville, 2020) which details how Sheffield Hallam University suggested that William Shakespeare, Virginia Woolf and William Blake feature on English literature courses not because their work is the 'best', but because they are white skinned and have benefitted from racial bias in curriculum selection and organisation over decades.

But then, perhaps Shakespeare did not write the works himself anyway (Pruitt, 2023).

Yet if a national examination is to be set, then all students need to be studying the same texts, and so there are choices to be made. Sehgal Cuthbert (2021: 62) calls this process 'arbitrary'. This debate is a product of ideological differences between a child-centred ideology and a cultural restorationist perspective. It also has echoes of Future 1 and Future 2 debates, with a set canon of literature which is to be handed down from generation to generation as part of cultural restorationist, Future 1 thinking, and the use of literature to 'illustrate a ready-formed opinion or [used] as a sort of therapeutic prompt' (Sehgal Cuthbert, 2021: 64) as a product of a child-centred, Future 2 approach to curriculum thinking.

This book is proposing that we move debates beyond these binaries and attempt to see how the knowledge gained through studying English can be empowering for young people as part of a powerful-knowledge-led Future 3 curriculum.

English as a powerful knowledge

English as a powerful knowledge is explored in an extended critical work by Robert Eaglestone (2021) in *Impact*. In this work, Eaglestone takes aim at the deficiencies of both powerful knowledge and E. D. Hirsch's *Cultural Literacy* (1988) as a way to explore the importance of English in a school curriculum. As he argues:

. . . .

Both 'powerful knowledge' and 'cultural literacy' rely on *one model of what knowledge is* … The kind of knowledge for which 'powerful knowledge' and 'cultural literacy' advocate is not the same as the kind of knowledge which underlies the study of literature. (Eaglestone, 2021: 9, emphasis in the original)

. . . .

The critique here is that English literature as a subject cannot be reduced to a list of facts for students to learn, as the Hirschian model implies. This would imply a Future 1 conception of the curriculum. Eaglestone's critique of powerful knowledge is linked to what he describes as the 'scientism' of the curriculum that just does not work for a subject like English. His issue is that there is not a clear conceptual link between the school subject and the academic discipline of English as researched at universities. If English knowledge is co-constructed between the text, teacher and student, then this makes notions of identifying 'better' knowledge a challenge. There can be no better knowledge derived from the university discipline as knowledge is being co-created in the class-room. Sehgal Cuthbert (2021: 65) adds, 'the subjectivity of the reader/ audience/pupil, as well as the artist/author, is integral, and not only in relation to the general motivation to learn. It plays a constitutive role in the knowledge itself.' Instead of seeing a correct way to engage with text, Hand (2021: 3) argues in the editorial introduction to Eaglestone's essay: 'the teaching of literature in schools should be guided ... by the deep understandings and signature pedagogies of the discipline of literary criticism'. These signature pedagogies involve many of the insights dis-cussed previously, including the need for discussion and engagement with the values dimension. According to this critique, this does not match the ideals of powerful knowledge.

Yet in the critique, he is putting both E. D. Hirsch's (1988) and Michael Young's (2008) conceptions of knowledge into the same category. As Chapter 3 showed, they are different, and that sets out the positions of Future 1 and Future 3. The key idea driving this book is that English offers a specialist knowledge to young people, and engagement with that knowledge enhances their capabilities.

If English is going to claim to be empowering for young people in some way, then the problem of choosing works needs to be resolved – to move beyond the culture wars that frame current discourse. Sehgal Cuthbert (2021: 70) offers a solution here, arguing that it is right to identify some form of canon, but that it 'is not set in stone, and its contents are revisable as literature itself develops; new genres and unearthing of previously unknown or neglected works can be included'. This notion of constantly working and reworking what might merit inclusion is allied to notions of 'better' knowledge, which is part of Michael Young's conception of powerful knowledge. The decision might not be taken 'on high' at university level, but by teachers in their own contexts, with their own students, thinking about which texts will best enhance and empower them.

Teacher voice

Table 6.1: Results of English teacher workshop

School A	School B	School C
Empathy and sensitivity – understanding of the human condition. Self-knowledge and understanding. Appreciation of the poetry, beauty, ornateness and simplicity of language. The power of language as a tool of communication. Interpretation and challenging established views.	Ability to explore the wider cultural and socio-economic impact of literacy. Deep informed understanding of the production and consumption of literature across time.	Language takes you to other places. It doesn't just reflect your own assumptions/prejudices, it challenges you with the views of others. Understanding how others use language/image to attempt to influence us. Building empathy. Literature grounds philosophy in the actual. Enables people to place themselves in time and place. English is profoundly interdisciplinary. The pleasure of deep immersion in something rather than a fast-food/InstaChat approach to life. Reading and reflecting on words/literature enhances attention, reason and reflection.

The English teacher cohorts were amongst the largest groups in the research study as the subject is compulsory to the age of 16, with many students choosing to stay on to study A level English. What is striking is how different these three conceptions are. The notion of using text to develop 'self-knowledge' comes through from School A and School C, as does the notion of developing values and empathy. Given its role as a core subject, it is hardly surprising that the teachers see themselves as holding a central role in the school – to develop competencies that will be useful across all subjects. School C explains that English is 'interdisciplinary'. This perhaps makes it difficult to express what makes it unique and what its specific role in the curriculum is. Much of what is explored here could be true of other subjects too – other languages are on the curriculum, so language is not a claim to uniqueness. The idea that students can gain pleasure from deep immersion could be a facet of every subject.

School B identifies a role for studying literature over 'time'; yet to do this effectively would involve studying similar types of literature from different time periods to see how ideas have evolved and changed. This was not an approach identified in the literature but could be part of a study into a particular literary tradition, such as the Gothic.

School C teachers offered the following vignette, a listing of ideas based on a soliloquy from *Hamlet*:

. . . .

What does 'To be or not to be ...' teach us? This could be connected philosophically to Descartes, etc. We could look at how metre and language link to the expression of character and to our own use of language to express emotion and thought. Bloom and the invention of modern consciousness. Early modern conceptions of melancholia. Connections to more recent paradigms for medicine and health – mental and physical. Connections to prelapsarian idylls and postlapsarian reality. Hamlet the adolescent and how that might connect to students' own views of themselves and life. Performance history of *Hamlet* and how that might connect to socio-historical conditions and political/religious assumptions at those times. The deviancy of despair and suicide. Christian constructions of despair. Discourses of disease and dis-ease. Renaissance idea of rhetoric and the limitations of 'words, words, words'.

. . . .

What is most striking about this vignette is that the teachers are discussing the outcomes of studying *Hamlet* in terms of increasing students' understanding of themselves. This is evident in ideas about expressing emotions and thoughts and views of the self. This relates clearly to the notion that knowledge in English literature is a co-construction between the words themselves and the student's reading of it. There are two types of substantive knowledge identified in this vignette. First is the broader setting of the specific text, including political and religious assumptions of the time, and Christian constructions of despair – what Eaglestone (2021) would describe as 'values'. This would also include contemporary understanding of mental health and suicide. The second type of substantive knowledge is that related to the analysis of language, with ideas such as 'metre', the rhythmic nature of verse, and how this helps convey meaning. The procedural knowledge is the ways in which students learn to analyse and interpret text, to take those 'words, words, words', identify the use of language and pick out key ideas, and then use this to build meaning. This process requires skilled teaching and practice over time.

Based on the input from teachers and the literature, the ways in which English could be considered a powerful knowledge for students could be expressed as:

❓ Knowledge of the greatest works of literature written in the English language. This includes an understanding of novels and plays, the impact that they have had in the past and continue to have in the present. The choice of this canon of works is constantly changing and teachers are key to deciding what is taught.

❓ Knowledge of the processes of eliciting meaning from a variety of texts. This includes the intentions of the writer as well as the ways in which the reader is responding to and making meaning from those words.

❓ Knowledge of the socio-cultural and political situations in which texts are initially created and how this may influence interpretation. This includes links to contemporary texts written in the same genre.

❓ Knowledge of how the meaning created through writing can assist in other subjects in the curriculum, including languages and humanities.

Conclusions: towards English capabilities

The English literature and language education discourse has been relatively quiet in exploring notions of powerful knowledge. This is due to many of the criticisms identified by Eaglestone (2021); there is not an identifiable 'core' knowledge of English beyond basic ideas around spelling and grammar. There is disagreement around whether there is, or even should be, a canon of great works that all students need to study. Given its role as a central subject on the curriculum, many teachers of English see its place in interdisciplinary terms; English becomes the gatekeeper to all other subjects where students are required to explore and express ideas through words.

Yet English can be considered a powerful knowledge. It is possible to express the ways in which the subject offers a unique knowledge contribution to young people. The substantive concepts include the rules of the English language: the ways in which sentences are constructed, the way in which a comma is placed and the ways in which this creates meaning (such as whether or not to include an Oxford comma in this sentence). It also includes a potentially endless knowledge of the text that is being studied. The context of the work, the writer, the time and place of publication, the socio-historical setting. The procedural knowledge of the subject is the ways in which any text can be scoured for meaning, and it is this knowledge that is tested when students are faced with a new piece of writing.

Together this helps the student to make meaning. Meaning is created through the interaction between the text and the student; it is therefore co-constructed. No two students will interpret the text in exactly the same way as each will bring themselves into it; a skilled teacher is key to this process. The extent to which the writer's intended meaning plays a part in this is still debated. It is this which makes English a powerful knowledge for young people, which in turn enhances their capacity to see the world in new ways.

For discussion

? Is there a canon of key texts that all students should study in school? If so, what is it and who gets to decide?

? What should (or should not) inform the choice of texts that students get to study in their school English lessons?

? To what extent should the writer's ideas inform how a student interprets their text? Should the writer's personal background and socio-economic setting inform the interpretation, or should students be able to make meaning using only the text in front of them?

? How can you tell if a student is getting better at English?

? What is the best way to assess students in English?

? What is the difference between literacy, oracy, listening, reading, literature and language? What order of priority should these take in the English classroom?

Chapter 7

What might make science a powerful knowledge?

The global pandemic of COVID-19 put science and scientists firmly in the media spotlight. Despite the claims in Chapter 1 – that we've 'had enough of experts' – it was the experts who devised the COVID vaccine that was rolled out across the world in 2022, earning its creators a Nobel Prize in 2023. The genetic sequence of the virus was posted online in January 2021, leading to a concerted effort to develop the vaccine from governments and pharmaceutical companies around the world. Relatively new technologies using mRNA were used on a massive scale, and to develop and test a new vaccine in eleven months was a global first. This shows the significance of scientific knowledge in the real world. Those scientists were working to a strict methodology to respond to a specific challenge.

'Science' can be defined by how you study something; therefore it is a procedural knowledge: a rigorous and replicable methodological approach. The different science subjects that come under its umbrella focus that activity into different areas: biology to the living world, physics to physical matter, chemistry to the makeup and behaviour of matter, and, more recently, computer science to the working of computer technologies.

Science as procedural knowledge

There are objectivist universal truths that can be theorised, tested and found to be true or dismissed as false, and it is this rigorous process that lies at the heart of science. In his book on the history of science, David

Wootton (2015: 517) calls science a 'research programme, [an] experimental method … [a] language of defeasible knowledge'. Eugene Anderson (2016: 56) argues that science is a 'dispassionate pursuit of truth', a 'human universal' to which all cultures have contributed in some form.

A scientific experiment carried out by a team working in a lab in India should get the same outcomes as the same experiment carried out in the same way in a lab in the USA. This replicability of results adds to the claims of truth that scientific experimentation can achieve. The key to new knowledge in science is in developing theories, finding a means to test them, and using the results to refine the theories and develop further experimentation. It is through this process that 'better' knowledge can be discovered. Old theories are disproved as new theories take their place.

Science as substantive knowledge

The scientific method provides the procedural knowledge that underpins all science, and the branches of science provide substantive knowledge of the various disciplines. Biology is the study of life, literally from the Greek βίος (bios) – 'life', and λογία (logia) – 'study of'. Chemistry is 'the study of the composition and properties of matter and how and why it undergoes change' (Gibney, 2018: 31) and physics is about matter, forces and energy. Erduran (2001: 583) identifies the unique nature of physics, citing the mathematical underpinning of the discipline:

. . . .

Unlike in chemistry and biology, in physics the tendency is towards mathematization, not classification of physical phenomena. Such differences … set apart chemistry from physics as a distinct domain of scientific inquiry.

. . . .

Yet these classifications are crude and there is much crossover, as Berglund and Reiss (2021: 190) explain:

. . . .

cells are to biology what atoms are to chemistry … and if cells are the foundation of biology, then what is inside the cells is on the boundary between biology and chemistry, which in itself has its own subject – biochemistry.

. . . .

Biochemistry is its own active and vibrant science discipline. Other scientific disciplines which provide substantive knowledge include earth science, geology, environmental science, psychology, medicine and engineering. Each of these has its own emphasis on what it is seeking to understand. With psychology it is the working of the human mind as it influences behaviour; with earth science it is the physical processes of the Earth. Social science has developed in an attempt to explore patterns in human behaviour (and this is examined in the humanities chapter). Despite the different substantive knowledge, the scientific method provides the unifying knowledge structure which underpins each strand.

Science knowledge in schools

Given the momentous impact that scientific discoveries have had on the progress of humanity, it is no surprise that science is a key component of school curricula around the world. As a core subject in the national curriculum in England it occupies a sacred space. It is the 'S' in STEM – alongside technology, engineering and maths – which recognises the employability of the subjects. In primary schools, students learn science, which in reality is a combination of a range of different scientific disciplines, but at secondary school there is a split into physics, chemistry and biology. The start of Key Stage 3, at 11 years old, is when students should start to be taught separate sciences by specialists, but of course this varies in practice. Often, younger secondary school students study science as some form of rotation between biology, chemistry and physics. At post-16 and university, a range of other sciences are available to study.

There is a challenge for teachers in schools over the extent to which lessons need to define both the contribution that science makes to the curriculum, as well as the unique role that each of the individual science subjects plays in education. Indeed, some have gone so far as to suggest that the standard presence of science in the curriculum as chemistry, physics and biology is itself outdated. Ravetz (2005: 11) proposes 'GRAIN – short for genomics, robotics, artificial intelligence and nanotechnology', to take into account more recent thinking and advances in scientific development.

A number of curriculum challenges exist regarding the teaching of science in secondary schools. Like many of the academic discourses outlined in this book, science is not immune to claims of white, male, Western hegemony. Much of what we consider science has been developed through Western (European and North American) thinking. This view of science is still evident in schools. What could make science more powerful for young people is a deeper appreciation of the struggle for evidence that has occurred over time rather than presenting the facts in front of them as simple truths.

One of the main challenges in school science lies in the large gap between it and what is researched in universities (e.g. Sturdy, 2021). University research is increasing in specialism and complexity. As Lyn Yates and Victoria Millar (2016: 306) explain, 'cutting edge topics cannot always be properly dealt with conceptually at the schooling stage of education, and ... there is not a simple linear path for building the foundations'. This is partly due to the increasingly complex nature of the experimentation used, but also to the level of mathematical competence required.

Even the selection of areas of study from the university discipline to introduce into schools is problematic. As Berglund and Reiss (2021: 192) complain of the biology curriculum:

> it is not obvious for students, indeed for teachers, why certain aspects of biology are in the curriculum and others are not. It looks rather as though the present curriculum is simply the result of a bit of a bun fight in which interested parties fight to get as much of their particular favourites in there.

A school science curriculum that fails to link to students' real world in some tangible way risks alienating them. This has been observed by Berglund and Reiss (2021: 194) when they identify:

> there is a decline in young people taking up studies in science ... They do not see the point of studying things that appear to them as a series of disconnected facts to be learned. In practice, too often the only point that they can discern is that they need to pass examinations.

This critique presents science lessons in terms of Future 1 thinking: a set of facts to be learnt and tested. This lack of engagement with the sciences has resulted in alternative conceptions of the science curriculum. In his chapter in *The Corruption of the Curriculum*, David Perks (2007) calls this 'science for citizenship'. This is where students become scientifically literate consumers of science; they are able to follow and comment on key scientific issues of the day rather than actively engaged in the creation of science for themselves through experimentation and practical classes.

A curricular model centred around relevance has been tried in various places across the world and over time. As Gareth Sturdy (2021: 228) points out, this:

. . . .

put a new emphasis on relevance to the student. It represented an attempt to teach how scientists develop knowledge but without the concepts through which that knowledge has been produced.

. . . .

In Australia, the physics curriculum was altered to reduce the amount of maths required and to incorporate more 'issues' that would be relevant and engaging to students. In their work reviewing this curriculum, Yates and Millar (2016: 306) interviewed a range of school and university physics teachers about this shift in emphasis. As they explain, 'These changes … led to what many interviewees described as a social science version of physics and was criticised by many as not being physics.'

This social science version of physics was developed to introduce the subject to a wider range of students and to engage and excite those who might otherwise have found it uninspiring. For example, part of the curriculum introduces students to electricity. Whereas a more traditional physics curriculum would have focused on the workings of the dynamo to create electricity and other means by which energy can be created, this new curriculum focused much more on renewable energy creation and its implications for energy security, climate change and future global sustainability. These issues are already in the news media and students' popular imagination. The problem is that if this concern leads the curriculum, then students are taken away from the physics of electricity generation. This sort of curriculum was heavily criticised by those interviewed in Yates and Millar's (2016: 306) research, with one university physicist even claiming:

. . . .

physics has been invaded by sociology and history and so the syllabi contained lots of reference to the socio-political forces … putting things into social context … is interesting but it's not physics.

. . . .

The curriculum debate outlined here echoes the Future 1 and Future 2 debate that Michael Young and Johan Muller (2010) identified. What the physicists in Yates and Millar's (2016) research seem to be advocating for is a knowledge-rich curriculum and, as such, they see any attempts to define school physics in terms of social potential as an 'invasion' – perhaps what others might call 'corruption' – as it takes students away from knowledge. This would be Future 2 curriculum thinking determining the nature of the school curriculum as a reaction to what could be perceived as the existing Future 1 curriculum – a body of academic knowledge that students need to learn. Defining what makes scientific knowledge powerful for young people could be a way to move beyond this dualism and ensure that subject content is taught rigorously, as well as shown to be relevant. This thinking is at the heart of a Future 3, powerful knowledge curriculum.

Science as a powerful knowledge

In many ways, the idea of conceptualising powerful knowledge suits science subjects well. Michael Young was himself a school chemistry teacher so would be well aware of the various curricular challenges outlined in the previous section. To achieve Future 3 curriculum thinking in science, teachers need to identify what makes it powerful for young people. Clearly, this will involve thoughts about the wider applicability of the knowledge beyond it being interesting in itself. However, this should come from a position of confidence in its own knowledge, without the need to stray into other subjects, such as geography, history or politics. The procedural knowledge of science is unique. It is robust hypothesis testing using a clear set of experimental rules that can be replicated to achieve the same results. Many writers have attempted to discuss the relevance of science in terms of its employability – such as enabling students to become doctors or engineers – but not all will go on to work specifically with scientific knowledge. The notion of scientific literacy provides a means to express what makes science knowledge powerful for a more general population, but there is a danger that this takes students away from the procedural knowledge that provides the foundations of science and the substantive knowledge developed within the discipline.

On what makes physics a powerful knowledge, Yates and Millar (2016: 304) argue:

> Neither school nor university physics teachers expect all students to achieve extensive expertise in physics … However they do want all students to (1) have some basic knowledge and induction into physics, (2) to learn and respect scientific method and reasoning and (3) to acquire respect (and preferably admiration) for the achievements of physics and the work of physicists and the contribution they make to the world.

This list seems to encapsulate many of the elements of powerful knowledge: a focus on the knowledge basis of the discipline, a knowledge of methodologies and ways of thinking that make science unique, and a broader appreciation of the purpose of knowledge.

To achieve the sorts of thinking that this powerful knowledge aspires requires students to be actively involved in 'doing' science rather than passive recipients of a load of scientific facts. In science classes, students should be conducting experiments, but time, safety concerns and budgets make this a challenge for some schools. If scientific literacy is the aim, then there is less need for experimentation. In some schools, experiments are conducted by the teacher in front of the class, but it is that live, tangible, participatory experimentation that is powerful in terms of developing young people's knowledge and understanding. Even this needs to be thought through carefully, however. In her work on the chemistry curriculum, Sibel Erduran (2001: 590) warns:

> students' experimentation in the chemistry laboratory is conventionally based on rote recipe following and is not representative of chemical inquiry that underlies what chemists do.

This would suggest that if science teachers are to engage students in experimentation in class, then it needs to be in the form of genuine enquiry in which students are actively engaged in setting up and planning the experiment rather than following a set 'recipe' provided by the teacher. Clearly, the extent to which this is possible will vary depending on the nature of the experiment and the age of the students, but active involvement in the scientific process, including critical reflection, seems to be an important element of what might make science powerful for young people.

In the wide-ranging *Second International Handbook of Science Education* (edited by Fraser et al., 2012), a chapter is given over to a critical take on science as a powerful knowledge: 'Curriculum integration: challenging the assumption of school science as a powerful knowledge' (Venville et al., 2012). They argue that powerful knowledge is unhelpfully 'insulated' within different disciplines and more integration between disciplines (even beyond the science disciplines) would render more power for young people. They illustrate this critique with an example:

> We observed students learning about the health of a nearby lake ... the content of science was not well insulated from the content from other school subjects including society and environment, English, mathematics, art and technology and enterprise ... The content varied and was determined by the interests of the individual students and the teacher ... The teachers justified these approaches by claiming that the students 'need stimulation' and that the approaches helped students to 'respond', gave them 'ownership', made them 'empowered' and 'connected to their own world', 'changed their attitudes' and, finally, resulted in them 'actively making decisions and changing their world'. (Venville et al., 2012: 745–746)

This class activity describes a deliberate attempt at cross-curricular teaching. The justification of the activity was around student needs, but these were framed by the idea of relevance – a Future 2 concern – rather than any intrinsic value of scientific study. They even suggest that disciplines very different to science, such as art, can play a role in this educational experience. As they go on to argue:

> the power of the knowledge taught and learned during the case study was that it was integrated and provided the students not only with powerful scientific knowledge, but also with powerful values in social and civic responsibility. (Venville et al., 2012: 746)

Yet there is a problem with their assertion. If the health of the lake is the object of study, and it is deliberately cross-curricular and following student interest, then it is not necessarily a 'science' activity at all. They have not explained how students were able to develop any scientific understanding. A lake absolutely can be studied scientifically, but without guidance from science specialists it is not known exactly what activities the students completed here that could be considered scientific.

The health of the lake was the specific parameter of study. Rigorous methodology could include the measuring of temperature, water sampling for phosphate and nitrate levels, and examination of the biological flora and fauna. These would teach students the procedural knowledge of science as well as the substantive knowledge of chemistry and biology needed to make sense of the findings. This is powerful knowledge in its own right, and should be valued, taught by a specialist and seen as such. What might then develop are broader educational capabilities – the ways in which the challenges of pollution might be communicated and the student agency required to address the needs of the environment. If other subjects were involved in this lake activity, then they too would help students to develop knowledge from their own discourse, such as using prose or poetry to develop empathy about water pollution, and this too might lead to enhanced capabilities.

The broader outcomes of the lake activity described here, such as civic responsibility, could be an expression of capabilities. But these will not be developed without a more rigidly structured approach to knowledge development. The real value of this activity could be sought by separating capabilities and powerful knowledge, and by promoting the intrinsic value of scientific study.

Teacher voice

Physics

Table 7.1: Results of physics teacher workshop

School A	School B	School C
Understand physical phenomena in the world and throughout the universe. Analyse and evaluate scientific claims to ensure accuracy and validity. Develop practical investigative skills to further explore encountered curiosities.	Physics describes both the large and the small. It describes how bodies communicate on both a local level (i.e. forces) and on a celestial level (i.e. space and gravity). Understanding of the properties of the objects that make up the world around us. The ability to interpret and analyse ideas graphically and mathematically.	Physics is an exciting intellectual adventure that inspires young people and expands the frontiers of our knowledge about nature. Physics generates fundamental knowledge needed for future technological advances. Physics contributes to the technological infrastructure needed to take advantage of scientific advances and discoveries. Physics is an important element in the education of chemists, engineers and computer scientists, as well as practitioners of the other physical and biomedical sciences. Physics extends and enhances our understanding of other disciplines, such as agricultural, biological, chemical, earth and environmental sciences, plus astrophysics and cosmology – subjects of substantial importance to all peoples of the world.

School A	School B	School C
		Physics improves our quality of life by providing the basic understanding necessary for developing new instrumentation and techniques for medical applications.

Teachers in School C offered the following vignette to illustrate the powerful nature of physics teaching:

. . . .

In Year 10 we cover the topic of electromagnetic radiation. This area of study reveals many characteristics of light in a rational and meas- urable way. It allows for the development of a firm understanding of how the sun, for example, provides visible light for photosynthesis and photovoltaic cells, UV light for vitamin D production but also skin cancer, infrared for warmth but also a runaway greenhouse effect. Each of these features is discussed in terms of the basic prop- erties of waves and how the differing wavelengths alter the behaviour of this huge spectrum of waves.

. . . .

The teachers in the physics departments express the power of physics knowledge in terms of its wider applicability to other areas, picking out the economy, medical developments and engineering. School A identifies the key role that physics plays in being able to investigate scientific claims to accuracy – a key capability that is developed through a good education in all subjects. School A also mentions 'investigative skills', which can be rephrased as the scientific method or procedural knowledge in terms of an important element of physics education. Perhaps of more value is the vignette about teaching ultraviolet waves to Year 10 (14–15-year-old) students. Whilst there are links to wider issues, such as global warming, what is clear is that the physics is at the core of these lessons, as the nature of the 'wavelengths' within the wider 'spectrum of waves' shows. This best illustrates the power of physics knowledge. From this knowledge base students can engage with the world; students' understanding of solar power use can help them to engage with the world in new ways, by actively seeking more sustainable energy supplies, for example, which develops their capabilities.

Biology

Table 7.2: Results of biology teacher workshop

School A	School B	School C
Structure and function of living organisms. Interactions within and between organisms and their non-living environment. Using knowledge and understanding to make decisions relevant to the conservation of natural capital.	Understanding of life systems – environment and body. Understanding the system of living things and how they work together. The similarities between how we (humans) work as a system and how the things around us work. By knowing this we can make better decisions about how we live.	A real-world subject which deepens both understanding and appreciation of the word around us. Through the study of the complex interactions between living organisms and their environment (internal and external), between different species and between individuals of the same species, the progress of life on Earth can be witnessed. Moving forward, the future of all species, including our own, can be predicted, explained and possibly changed for the better.

School C's vignette:

. . . .

In Year 10, students were asked to evaluate the use of a new drug (Drug C) based on statements given about its effectiveness, its cost per dose and its side effects in comparison with two other existing drugs (A and B). To complete this exercise, the students needed to be able to weigh up evidence from a variety of sources and presented in different formats. Having evidence to support choices is vital; that the evidence has come from a reliable source (or large sample size) adds to its weight. Students are often concerned about getting it 'right', but it is the process that they go through to reach the decision that is key here.

. . . .

School A references 'natural capital': the idea that nature is able to provide value to humans through the provision of clean air and water, as well as more tangible economic resources. School C links different elements of the substantive knowledge of the subject. The idea of the powerful knowledge of biology as somehow giving students an 'appreciation' of the natural world is laden with values – who decides what is and what is not to be valued is not explored. For the biology teachers here, the idea of using the scientific method to explore the natural world is not considered; it is almost a given. The vignette is expressed in terms of a real-world experiment of drug testing. Here, it is students' ability to weigh up evidence, obtained through scientific rigour, and draw conclusions that shows the power of the scientific method.

Chemistry

Table 7.3: Results of chemistry teacher workshop

School A	School B	School C
Universal understanding of processes and properties of everyday things that occur around us all the time. Consequential knowledge obtained about effects of processes (e.g. pollution). Scope for important, ground-breaking discoveries. Making links between key theory and wider application in industry, environment and the world around us. Vast array of multifaceted skills obtained: analytical, observational, qualitative, quantitative, mathematical.	Knowledge of the building blocks of matter. Understanding of the wide world and how things work. The importance of cause and effect; reactions create something new. Links to real-world calculations of yield – important for industry. Understanding of climate change and the greenhouse effect. Links to the food industry – process of chemical composition of nutrients.	We need excellent chemistry teaching to produce our future scientists, but teaching chemistry is not just about providing knowledge. It is about the protection and promotion of scientific transparency and ensuring that facts and evidence are not obscured by ideology, no matter how inconvenient. In a world of fake news, there has never been a more urgent need to infix scientific literacy and educe critical thought from all our students.

School C's vignette:

. . . .

The importance of chemistry to society cannot be understated in terms of its contribution to the social, economic, technological and environmental aspects of modern life. Breakthroughs in medical science have historically been led by chemists, from Pasteur to Sanger. It was a chemist, Rosalind Franklin, who discovered the structure of DNA. Sarah Gilbert is a biochemist who has led the AstraZeneca team to produce Oxford's COVID vaccine. Our comfortable lifestyles are made possible by chemists: fabrics, plastics and food production are all under the chemistry umbrella. Chemists are working hard to save the planet: it was a photochemist, Giacomo Luigi Ciamician, who made the first solar cells. Carbon capture and storage, ozone chemistry, acid rain, the chemistry of the oceans ... the answers all lie within this central science.

. . . .

The vignette from the chemistry teachers seems to echo much of the power of school science. Although these teachers did not quite stick to the brief (to give an example of something they have taught), they use the space to make an impassioned plea for scientific literacy – for students to be able to identify accuracy in truth claims. The teachers from School C chose to focus on famous chemists and their discoveries; this gives the subject personality and makes it about people and their discoveries, humanity and its search for truth. Yes, chemistry is an objectivist subject about searches for truth, but it is people who are behind this process. It would be interesting to know how many of those people mentioned in their expression of powerful knowledge feature in chemistry lessons in their school, and the extent to which scientific literacy involves students conducting practical experiments.

The teachers here have examined the ways in which the sciences could be expressed as a powerful knowledge. The extent to which the teachers pick out elements of the substantive knowledge of their subject or lean more towards the procedural knowledge of the scientific method varies both within the strands of science but also between school teacher teams. This lack of consistency between teachers suggests that there is more work to be done on identifying and communicating the value of the science subjects.

Conclusions: towards science capabilities

Based on the literature and the voices of the teachers in the study, the powerful knowledge of science could be expressed as:

❓ A rigorous and replicable methodology following strict rules of knowledge production. Experiments allow scientists to replace previous theories with new ones as science advances. Students should have opportunities to design and carry out their own controlled experiments, and to present and analyse the results.

❓ The substantive knowledge of science comes from the different specialisms: physics covers matter, laws and astronomy; chemistry covers processes and properties; biology focuses on the living world. The possible content here is vast, but teachers are key to selecting and recontextualising the best knowledge for students to engage with in the classroom.

❓ Students should also be able to critique the scientific knowledge claims of others and discern science fact from science fiction.

Science is a core component of the school curriculum as it provides students with much powerful knowledge, through which a range of capabilities can develop. The main way in which the science subjects explored here – biology, physics and chemistry, as well as those mentioned but not explored directly (computer science and psychology) – can be expressed as powerful is in terms of procedural knowledge. The scientific method is about rigorous hypothesis testing, changing variables and seeking objective truths, and it is this that helps students to identify and address falsehoods. Venville et al.'s (2012) chapter in the *Second International Handbook of Science Education* was critical of the idea of a discernible powerful knowledge of science, instead seeking to define science's power through integration with other subjects in the curriculum. This does not seem to chime with the rest of the literature, nor with the research data presented here; the teachers in this study were able to identify a range of substantive knowledge that was significant for students to grasp if they are to study something scientific.

For discussion

? Which of the science subjects are most important for young people to engage with in the classroom?

? In younger year groups, is it better to teach combined science or the discrete disciplines from the start? What are the opportunities and challenges of each curricular model?

? Why is it important for science teachers to keep up to date with academic developments in their subject? How will you achieve this in the classroom?

? What makes hands-on experiments in the science lab (or in the field) powerful for young people?

? Could you work up a curriculum vignette for school chemistry to showcase the significance of the subject for young people?

? Could you rework and define the expression of powerful knowledge shown in this chapter? What is missing? What could be rephrased?

Chapter 8

What might make the humanities a powerful knowledge?

The police had been called to a disturbance outside a school in West Yorkshire in March 2021. On arrival, they saw a horde of angry parents chanting 'shame on you' and calling for the sacking of one of the teachers. It soon became a media frenzy, with banks of photographers and film crews recording the unfolding scene. Batley Grammar School had become the centre of national attention. The previous day, a religious education (RE) teacher had shown a cartoon image of the Prophet Muhammad to a class of students. This is seen as a deeply offensive act in Islam. In the town of Batley, 41% of the population is Muslim, and two-thirds of students in the school itself are from ethnic minority backgrounds (Duell and Wright, 2021). The teacher in question showed the image deliberately, even telling the class that some will find it offensive. Five months prior to this event a teacher in Paris was murdered for doing something similar, and in 2015 a gunman opened fire on the offices of *Charlie Hebdo* magazine, which first published the cartoons that were being shown, killing twelve people.

Later that day, the head teacher was paraded on the news to give an 'unequivocal' apology (Duell and Wright, 2021) and the teacher involved was suspended. The teaching materials were removed and schemes of work changed. Although the media interest ended as quickly as it had erupted, the national headlines once again ignited debates about freedom of speech, and what should and should not be taught to students in schools – the central theme of this book.

The controversial cartoons are readily available online for anyone who chooses to search for them, and yet they are a curricular peculiarity. The images are only offensive to students from one religious group and there are not equivalents in other religions; the Christian God is depicted in many forms. This makes it culturally sensitive. The choice of teaching resource was designed to provoke discussion and engender a reaction from students. The cartoons exist; these images are the sort of thing that could be shared on social media, and, presumably, the teacher felt that it was important to show them so that everyone could understand what they were talking about. The teacher was preparing their students for life in the real world where they may come across these images for themselves and was helping them to manage their possible reactions.

Local Muslim community leader Mohammad Sajad Hussain wrote an open letter in which he said how 'deeply hurt' he was by the 'insulting caricatures', but the National Secular Society argued that the protest was an 'attempt to impose an Islamic taboo onto a school'. Its chief executive, Stephen Evans, as reported in the *Mail Online* (Duell and Wright, 2021), argued:

. . . .

Teachers must have a reasonable degree of freedom to explore sensitive subjects and enable students to think critically about them. And the school's weak response will fuel a climate of censorship, which is brought on by attempts to force society as a whole to accommodate unreasonable and reactionary religious views.

. . . .

This episode brings into sharp focus the important role that teachers have in curriculum thinking and getting the balance right between provocation to engender discussion and causing deliberate offence. This book argues that teachers need to be trusted as curriculum makers, and a key part of this is knowing their students. Whilst no teacher should be censored, as this would be a form of curriculum corruption, cultural sensitivities must be taken into consideration as part of the curriculum making process. Teachers are in very trusted and influential positions.

Humanities in the curriculum

The subjects which make up the humanities all take people as their object of study, using a range of methodologies. In schools, these subjects would include geography, history, RE and sometimes sociology, business studies, classical civilisation, economics and politics. There is a distinction to be made between humanities and social sciences, although there is considerable overlap between them. As a Fellow of the British Academy, Professor Iain McLean (2018) explains, 'the key difference is that humanities are (mostly) interested in the unique; social sciences are (mostly) interested in the general'. The difference between social sciences and humanities is one of methodology. Sociology was originally described as a social science, but now the description can encompass subjects like economics. As shown in Chapter 7, if science is defined by its methodology, so the social sciences apply the rigour of the scientific method to the study of people. This would include using big data to apply statistical analysis and using game theory to predict and explain group behaviours. Humanities rely much more on narrative methodologies and individual stories.

Social science would fall under the umbrella term of STEM subjects, identified for their supposed access to top professions. Arguably, a subject community would want to brand themselves as part of the STEM group in order to attract more students rather than allying themselves with the humanities. Sociology, economics and geography, as school subjects, have often tried to do this. These distinctions are unhelpful. Geography is defined by what is being studied rather than how it is being studied; it can be a humanity if it is focusing on behavioural approaches of people and place, but equally it can be a social science when looking at global scale population demographics, and even a science when studying the physical geography of landscape change. Linguistics, the study of which can help inform languages education, sits right across the boundary of humanities and social science.

There is also a challenge of subject identity within RE. This book uses RE (for religious education), Ruth Ashbee (2021) calls it religious studies (RS) and it has even been called religion philosophy and ethics (RPE) or the same words in a different combination (such as PRE) in some schools. The name of a subject matters as it provides students with a sense of identity about what they are learning. If we go with RS or RE, it is one of the few subjects (along with PE) that has the word 'education' or 'studies' in its title, showing its educative importance.

One of the challenges in schools is that often the subjects of geography, history and RE are combined to form humanities, particularly at Key Stage 3 (11- to 14-year-olds). This not only reduces the amount of time a student is able to spend studying the individual subjects but also may mean that they are not taught by a specialist teacher; a history teacher is not able to teach geography in the same way that a geography teacher can. This can have a detrimental effect on student uptake of the subjects following Year 9 'options' (there is a discussion on this in relation to school geography in Bustin, 2019). Science teachers have raised similar criticisms of generic science lessons in schools rather than offering students specialist teaching in biology, chemistry and physics.

Humanities knowledge(s)

Each of the three main humanities subjects that are the focus of this chapter (geography, history and RE) all educate students about people, yet each has its own specialist claims to truth and power. RE takes values, faith and belief as its central focus. Ruth Ashbee (2021: 83) identifies that 'religion presents perhaps humanity's oldest search for meaning beyond ourselves'. Rania Hafez (2021: 174), in her contribution to *What Should Schools Teach?*, defines the subject as 'one of the compasses we humans have used to chart our moral progress; faith, as much as cognition, has played its part in moral and cultural flourishing'. The subject has no single university discourse to draw from but relies on a range of university disciplines – such as philosophy, theology, and even politics and economics – for its knowledge. RE has a range of curricular aims. As Hafez (2021: 179) proposes:

> First is to teach the students the history and content of the faiths that have helped shape human thinking and our modern world ... Second, RE, along with other subjects such as literature, has the role of inducting students into the ancient and ongoing philosophical debates around the nature of what it is to be human.

These curricular aims show the multidisciplinary approach to the methods of RE, drawing on literary criticism and historical analysis. At the centre of RE are the world's major religions, which have developed over thousands of years. The sets of religious teachings are often based on ancient texts which students are able to read (in translation) and interpret. As such, knowledge is co-constructed between the texts and rules of the religion being studied and the young person reading and interacting with those texts. There is a sense of subjective knowledge too, with meaning being imposed onto a series of objects which then become symbolic. Students are able to interact with these to make meaning. The subject has a horizontal knowledge structure, so different topics can be studied in any order, and it does not rely on previous knowledge for progression.

The substantive knowledge of RE (according to Ashbee, 2021) therefore includes theology (such as sacred texts), the norms and values of the religions being studied, and religious teachings and their interpretations. There is also substantive knowledge of philosophy, with knowledge of concepts such as the just war theory and arguments for the existence of God. There is knowledge of historical, social and political groups and ideas and how they shape contemporary discourse. The substantive knowledge of RE is also informed by social science ideals, such as being able to use and interpret big data and its associated statistical analysis, such as census data on religious observance of a population.

The procedural knowledge of RE is about the construction of arguments and being able to draw on evidence to back up those arguments. It is less about coming up with answers to difficult questions and more about the process by which answers can be structured. There is a logical sequence to the creation of philosophical arguments, and this is something that needs to be taught as procedural knowledge. The manipulation of data and statistics is also a procedure that can be taught.

There are some curricular challenges specific to the teaching of RE. As Mary Myatt (2018: 194) is keen to point out, 'RE is not religious instruction', so although there is a strong values dimension to the subject, it involves values clarification rather than values transmission. Allied to this is the stance taken by the teacher. As she argues, 'the personal beliefs of the teacher or pupil is irrelevant' (Myatt, 2021: 194). There is a debate too about which religions should be included in the curriculum. In the 2021 census, the number of people in the UK identifying as Christian fell below 50% of the population for the first time to 46.5% (Office for National Statistics, 2022), and second to this are those who identify as having no religion at all (37.2%). Other world views such as humanism are also on the rise. According to the Understanding Humanism website, 5% of the population self-identify as humanists.[1] This suggests that there could be a place for humanism in curricular discussions.

---

1   See https://understandinghumanism.org.uk/what-is-humanism/how-many-humanists-are-there.

Another challenge specific to RE is the way in which it can be used as a vehicle for relationships and sex education (RSE) rather than seen as valuable knowledge in its own right. Schools are required to teach RSE, but where similar conversations occur in RE lessons, it can be framed within a religious setting. A more appropriate place for RSE might be PSHE lessons or biology lessons. Using RE lessons in this way could be an example of Future 2 thinking, where a subject becomes the vehicle for sex education.

Geography has been described as 'one of humanity's big ideas' (Bonnett, 2008: 1). Studying it can encompass a wide range of methodologies from objectivist scientific approaches to interpretations of literature; what unites the disparate methods is that they all help students to understand something about place. A geomorphologist studying rates of coastal erosion on a cliff is as much a geographer as a person studying artistic representations of landscapes. The subject is traditionally split into physical and human geography, and even at GCSE level students will sit separate examination papers in those two sides of the subject.

The substantive knowledge of geography is therefore potentially vast, and in schools it is typically divided into a series of topics – such as urban geography and coastal geography – which are horizontally structured (to use Bernstein's (2000) descriptor). Strong subject organisations for teachers – such as the Geographical Association with its journal *Teaching Geography* – help to discuss and challenge what is taught in schools. The exam boards also select topics for inclusion, which influences the curriculum, and this tends towards a similar set of topics being taught (such as urban and global development, tourism, migration, glaciation, coasts, rivers and climate change). The procedural knowledge of geography is the range of methods which can help students to make sense of the world. Many of these are found in other subjects, from science to literature. Geographers are adept at fieldwork and getting students to make measurements and observations in the real world, although it is not the only subject that offers fieldwork; biologists will often take students to collect real-world data in the field. Mapping in all its forms, from interpretations of cartographic information through to analysis of big data using geographical information systems digital maps is a key part of the procedural knowledge of the subject.

Given the desire to avoid the trap of lists of facts (capital cities, longest rivers, and so on which would be Future 1 thinking) and the corrupting influence of just teaching values without any engagement in the background knowledge needed to make sense of it all (Future 2 thinking), it was geography educationists who led the research into the application of powerful knowledge. This was through various curriculum development projects and research, the story of which is explained in various publications (Solem et al., 2013; Young and Lambert, 2014; Bustin, 2019) and earlier in this book.

If geography is about places, then history is about time, and the events that have shaped people and places over the grand sweep of human existence. Meaning in history is made through the interpretation of evidence, and this can take many forms. As Ashbee (2021: 79) explains:

> the creation of meaning in the subject relies heavily on the interpretation of the knower, whilst simultaneously being informed by the evidence. That evidence is always, and necessarily, incomplete.

As such, knowledge is co-constructed between the available evidence and the person interpreting it. The evidence can be first-hand narrative accounts but also articles, photographs and artefacts. Through this interpretation, a narrative about the past can be constructed. This might involve small-scale stories from individual people in the past that feed into a much wider story, and this change of scale can be engaging for students. As Mary Myatt (2021: 175) explains, 'it is the relationship between the grand narrative and the intimate or local story that has the power to draw pupils in'.

Horizontally structured, the substantive knowledge of the subject potentially contains every event that has ever occurred in the past, as well as the concepts that help to make sense of events and changes over time, such as war or revolution. In her chapter in *What Should Schools Teach?*, Christine Counsell (2021: 157) explores the types of knowledge in history lessons and observes:

> Broadly speaking ... the various types of disciplinary knowledge adopted by history teachers in England have fallen into three categories: (a) types of historical question and corresponding accounts; (b) using evidence and (c) interpretations.

This contains a mix of both substantive and procedural knowledge, and contributes to the grand aspirations of 'historiography': the ways in which the academic discipline develops new knowledge by asking questions and using sources to answer them.

In choosing topics to teach, Counsell (2021) reminds us that each nation will have key moments which define it, and this shared history naturally forms part of the selection. Ashbee (2021) differentiates between 'established' substantive knowledge, which would include the dates of significant events (such as coronations), and 'contested' substantive knowledge, which would include anything subject to argument and debate, such as the causes of the Second World War. Students can enter into those discussions as part of their history lessons.

The procedural knowledge of history involves the analysis of sources from the past as well as using these to construct arguments and debates. In a classroom, young people are not using original sources, but a carefully curated set of artefacts that the history teacher has chosen to present as part of the recontextualisation process.

Getting the balance right between substantive and procedural knowledge is the key to successful history teaching. An overfocus on learning substantive knowledge tends towards Future 1 curriculum thinking, learning dates and events by rote as if they are somehow set in stone. Just focusing on source analysis out of context is akin to Future 2 thinking, where the skill of interpretation becomes the end point of a lesson. In his contribution to *The Corruption of the Curriculum*, Chris McGovern (2007) argues that 'source analysis' became the central tenet of the 'New History' curriculum, which was designed to make history more accessible to young people in the late 1990s and prevailed until the knowledge turn of the 2010s. It was a central part of the GCSE assessment; students were shown cartoons or newspaper clippings to interpret without building into a wider historical narrative. Students had a mixed-up sense of chronology and no awareness of significant national and global events. McGovern (2007) cites a Cambridge lecturer who complained that their students were arriving for undergraduate study without really knowing anything.

Humanities as a corrupt curriculum

Given the potential vastness of the knowledge base of RE, geography and history, and the need to select something to teach to students in schools, the humanities subjects were accused of being corrupted. Alex Standish

(2007: 29) suggests in his geography chapter in *The Corruption of the Curriculum*:

Students are not only being taught about how the world is, but how it ought to be. These global values include the natural environment, cultural tolerance, social justice and equality.

His concern is that instead of being taught knowledge of the world in order to help students make up their own mind about global issues, which would be Future 3 curriculum thinking, they were being told what to think and how to respond to complex issues – a Future 2 approach. This is something that Morgan and Lambert (2005: 62) have called 'morally careless' teaching. This concern is echoed in RE teaching, as Hafez (2021: 186) argues: 'the approach to RE to date has been muddled and has confused pedagogical and intellectual aims with other wider social aims'. RE lessons have become the place to discuss Future 2 concerns like social integration rather than to understand the major world religions, ethics and philosophy. In history education, Future 2 themes such as gender and social diversity become filters through which to explore events in the past (McGovern, 2007). When this is done uncritically, with the aim to make a particular point about the topic under scrutiny, this can affect the way in which students perceive and interact with the past.

Michael Young's (1971) discussion of knowledge 'of the powerful' (his Future 1 position) is particularly pertinent in the humanities, given the role that people play in formulating the discourse. Whose knowledge is it that we are presenting to students? This has become an issue of contemporary concern and has the potential to skew the narratives that are key to knowledge creation. History can be used to promote nationalism by focusing on the successful nation-building elements of the past whilst omitting the defeats or the dark periods of history. School geography has been accused of presenting a white male voice, which is inherently racist, to students. In their introduction to *Geography*, Danny Dorling and Carl Lee (2016: 50) assert:

Successful assertions of power, such as that of Britain, framed geography into the 20th century, and early school geography books in Britain were underpinned with a social Darwinist pecking order of racial superiority.

There has been a 'deafening silence' around discussions of race in the geography curriculum (as discussed in Puttick and Murrey, 2020), but this is beginning to change (e.g. Morgan and Lambert, 2023). There has been a renewed effort in schools to 'decolonise' the geography curriculum, to increase the range of voices presented and to paint a more holistic picture of the world. Some excellent articles in the journal *Teaching Geography* have been exploring this (e.g. Milner, 2020). Black History Month has become a key feature in schools, during which a deliberate attempt is made to focus on the contribution that Black scholars have made in areas of historical discourse, as well as notable Black figures from the past whose stories have gone untold. But, as Christine Counsell (2021) warns, this should not be a tokenistic add-on to what is already being taught; instead, Black narratives should be integrated into all areas of the curriculum. She also reviews a range of attempts that teachers have made to focus on the histories of students in the classroom. In their ethnically diverse London school, with a significant proportion of children with Somali heritage, Mohamud and Whitburn (2014) changed their curriculum to add Somali histories to engage those students. This is a deliberate attempt at personalising the curriculum.

In multicultural humanities classrooms, effective curriculum making would ensure that the stories of all the students are being told in a way that fully engages them with the subject knowledge and does not treat it as tokenism. There is a challenge with this, of course. If Somali history is illuminating and worthy of teaching for one class with a high percentage of Somali children, then surely it has something to offer to classes with no Somali children. This presents classroom teachers with specific challenges in deciding the appropriate balance between grand narratives (and major events) and more specific individual stories.

As I have shown in the introduction with my own anecdote of fieldwork in New Zealand, the drive to diversify voices in the curriculum has been a well-meaning but often quite confused activity. This process does not mean replacing science with folk narratives but seeks to understand where those narratives come from and why they are important in offering a greater understanding of the world. In his work on the New Zealand history curriculum, Mark Sheehan (2021) discusses the notion of the 'culturally responsive' curriculum, which aims to support teachers in navigating the complexities of Māori histories. Yet he identifies difficulties, as he explains:

> Without historical knowledge of the difficult features of New Zealand's past, the culturally responsive curriculum will simply provide a series of vague, superficial, ambiguous guidelines that contribute little to young people being able to make authentic connections between the past and the present. (Sheehan, 2021: 204)

For him, substantive knowledge of the past is key to helping students to engage with the 'difficult' aspects of their nation's stories, which in turn helps students to place themselves within a broader historical timeline.

Despite these challenges, well-constructed RE, geography and history curricula can give students the knowledge needed to engage critically with values, and it is this that could be at the heart of powerful knowledge of the humanities subjects.

Humanities as powerful knowledges

Michael Young was a school chemistry teacher before becoming an educational sociologist and, as such, his ideas around powerful knowledge seem to apply well to the sciences but less so to other areas of the curriculum. Despite this, it is the humanities that have seen the greatest body of subsequent work exploring powerful knowledge; the story of school geography has already been told in this book. In history education, a significant contribution is *Knowing History in Schools: Powerful Knowledge and the Powers of Knowledge*, edited by Arthur Chapman (2021a). This multi-authored book was born from a 2017 British Educational Research Association symposium which bought together a series of history educationists and Michael Young himself to explore the ideas. In his chapter, Sheehan (2021) sets some parameters for exploring the powerful knowledge of history. As he argues:

> Establishing what is powerful knowledge in the school [history] curriculum largely depends on whether the primary purpose of the subject is seen to be providing young people with disciplinary informed, evidence-based approaches to the past that develop

critical thinking; or if history is seen to make a wider societal contribution to developing young people's understandings of questions to
do with identity, diversity, social cohesion and belonging. (Sheehan,
2021: 204)

. . . .

In this quotation he sets out the contentions between the various
futures. A Future 1 informed curriculum would see the learning of dates
and facts as its primary aim. Progression would be based on the number
of facts that have been accrued over time. Concepts, such as 'the Church'
or 'war', would be presented to students uncritically as a set of ideas to
learn. Events, unfolding over time, would be regarded as a set story from
a definitive viewpoint. A Future 2 informed curriculum would be focused
on, as Sheehan suggests here, a range of social concerns like identity and
diversity; however, these then become the central driver of the curriculum, devoid of the historical knowledge and understanding on which
they can be based. The overlap that Sheehan (2021) identifies here is the
space in which the Future 3 curriculum can be envisioned.

In her chapter in *Knowing History in Schools*, Alison Kitson (2021) identifies
the ways in which powerful knowledge can be useful for young people,
which in turn can help develop their capabilities (although she does not
use the language of capabilities). This work was informed by Alaric
Maude's (2016) types of geographical knowledge, discussed in Chapter 3.
This is shown in Table 8.1.

Table 8.1: The ways in which powerful knowledge might be useful to history students (from Kitson, 2021: 43)

What powerful knowledge might enable students to do	Examples of how history might contribute to these aims
Discover new ways of seeing the world today	By helping students to understand that: ▪ things have not always been as they are now ▪ decisions and developments in the past shape the present and future ▪ things do not happen because they are inevitable ▪ people in the past (and in the present) were/are diverse and understanding their actions is difficult but important.
Engage in society's conversations and debates about itself	By helping students to understand that: ▪ history can help us to understand the present ▪ history can help us to think about the future ▪ a longer perspective (that is, 'bigger pictures' or frameworks) can help us to identify approaches to complex issues in the present.
Understand the grounds for accepting or rejecting knowledge claims	By helping students to understand that: ▪ there is a relationship between a claim and the weight of evidence behind that claim ▪ 'history' and 'the past' are different. History is deliberately constructed by someone after the event ▪ the past is interpreted in different ways by different people.

The three ideas in the first column could be seen as history capabilities; the capabilities that students develop from studying a rigorous history curriculum. The powerful knowledge which can develop those capabilities is explored further in the second column. Many of the ideas in the second column have been considered in this chapter, such as the role of evidence in making claims of historical truths, but we haven't discussed the idea of contributions to the present and the future. According to this school of thought, studying the past will help young people to understand both the present and the future. This would need to be made explicit to students, with tangible links made between the topic in question (such as the Tudors) and our contemporary world, such as comparing attitudes towards the Church in Tudor times to those of today. One of the expressions of the powerful knowledge of geography is that it has a strong futures element, particularly with ideas around environmental sustainability. For historians to claim that the 'future' is a deliberate part of their knowledge is different to the ideas explored in Ashbee (2021), Counsell (2021) and Myatt (2021).

RE can also claim to be a powerful knowledge for young people in terms of the ways in which knowledge of the world, ethics, philosophy and religion is used by students to engage with values. Although they are not engaging with the discourse around powerful knowledge directly, the writers in *Big Ideas for Religious Education*, edited by Barbara Wintersgill (2017), propose a set of key principles that can be used to conceptualise a new RE curriculum. Hafez (2021: 179–180) summarises these in the following objectives:

- to develop in students an appreciation of religion as a distinct conceptual framework of knowledge as well as a manual for living for 'believers',

- to develop students' knowledge and understanding of the tenets, practices and contemporary manifestations of key faith traditions,

- to develop students' understanding of the way world religions have influenced and been shaped by various elements of the human experience, including our knowledge in history, philosophy, science, art and culture,

- to develop students' critical approaches and enquiry skills as they explore and evaluate religious beliefs, doctrines and philosophies.

The types of knowledge here are similar to ideas expressed earlier about the role of historical sources. What is different is the direct expression of an emotional response to knowledge – the first bullet point talks of an 'appreciation'. This is comparable with Geoff Hinchliffe's (2006) humanities capabilities, explored in Chapter 4, as he suggests that humanities students need to develop 'concern' for others as a key capability. Directly teaching students to appreciate or to be concerned about something is a challenge in itself and, if it can be done, it tends towards Future 2 thinking. Teaching students knowledge which is likely to elicit concern and appreciation would be Future 3 thinking.

A key part of powerful knowledge is that 'better' knowledge could replace established ideas. In science this involves a direct replacement of one theory with another as new discoveries are made, but it is a more complex process in the humanities. Proponents of decolonising the curriculum could claim to be attempting to provide 'better' knowledge by showing that accepted narratives are often the result of inherent bias (such as the debates around the use of the Burgess land use model, as discussed in Chapter 1). Whether these ideas are in fact 'better' knowledge or simply different but equally acceptable versions of history (or geography or RE) is contestable, but what is key for a powerful-knowledge-led Future 3 curriculum is that knowledge is not static and always open to debate.

Teacher voice

Geography is omitted from this section as work from the GeoCapabilities project was used as the exemplar. Instead, the geography teachers were asked to critically reflect on the frameworks offered by Lambert and Maude and work up another vignette of powerful knowledge in action. Examples of these can be found on the GeoCapabilities project website.[2]

---

2   See www.geocapabilities.org.

RE

Table 8.2: Results of RE teacher workshop

School A	School B	School C
Increasing factual knowledge of the views of major world religions on the big metaphysical and ethical questions. Nurturing students' own viewpoints on these issues and fostering their spiritual awareness through challenging viewpoints.	Rigorous analysis of concepts and arguments and coming to conclusions. 'Factual' and descriptive knowledge of alternate schools of thought/faiths and contexts. Putting together concepts and ideas to compare and contrast, and argue and debate.	To understand the world and our place in it from differing 'transcendent' perspectives. This is in contrast to the 'immanent frame' of the rest of the curriculum.

Although each set of teachers has offered a different way to express what makes RE a powerful knowledge, there are similarities, in line with the ways in which the literature explores the role of RE in the curriculum. Both School A and School B identify factual knowledge of world religions as core substantive knowledge, but the idea of confronting differing and challenging viewpoints and developing arguments to engender discussion is also key, and this was identified as procedural knowledge. School C focuses on the key difference between RE and other subjects as one of perspective; RE allows a student to step away from an issue and explore it from multiple perspectives, including ones of religious faith. This is part of the philosophical thinking that was alluded to in the literature.

RE teachers from School C offered a vignette:

. . . .

Teaching of the parables of Dives and Lazarus and the sheep and the goats to Year 9: What seems like a dry, ancient (and in the latter case repetitive) text can be lifted by an examination of the variety of perspectives from within each contrasted with that of Jesus' motive in telling the parable. The ultimate 'end' of the stories pointing beyond this world to the ideas of salvation and the Kingdom of Heaven (transcendence). The validity or otherwise of these perspectives is, as always, up for grabs.

. . . .

This vignette focuses on the substantive knowledge of RE, in this case a Christian Bible story being taught to Year 9 (13–14-year-old) students. Here it is not taught as fact (a Future 1 position), and nor is it used as a vehicle to deliver something deemed more worthy (a Future 2 position). It is an illustration of Future 3 thinking; students are introduced to the 'dry', 'ancient', 'repetitive' text (the substantive knowledge of RE) but from differing perspectives. This enables discussion about interpretations of the text and the motivation behind the parable. An example of that 'transcendence' is also illustrated, linking the story to bigger ideas about God. The final sentence shows a key idea of powerful knowledge: RE does not teach students what to think or how to respond but explores a range of ideas; it discusses and debates.

Based on this, the ways in which RE can be considered a powerful knowledge can be expressed as follows:

❓ Descriptive knowledge of world religions and faith traditions, including prevalence, significant cultures and traditions, and the impact on people (such as providing a manual for 'believers', as well developing an understanding of impacts on cultures, art, science and faith practices) around the world and over time.

❓ Knowledge of philosophical, spiritual and ethical debates, including evidencing, construction of arguments and arriving at one's own conclusions whilst understanding alternatives.

History

Table 8.3: Results of history teacher workshop

School A	School B	School C
This subject helps us understand human behaviour – individual, group and mass behaviour – in the context of its time. It also helps us to understand how ideas develop, how institutions function and how cultures evolve. Studying this against a chronological framework is especially useful when trying to understand causation and change.	This subject is about people and the situations we have found ourselves in over time. History allows us to see the consequences of the decisions that people have taken.	History offers a unique study of the entirety of our human past, from the political to the philosophical, theological, artistic, scientific and far beyond; and, if studied in its own terms, free from the dictates of present assumptions, it allows a critical engagement with the rich diversity of human lived experience. This brings the imaginative joy of going beyond the narrow constraints, assumptions and political preoccupations of our own very particular twenty-first-century lives. It allows students to contextualise and treat with scepticism the reductive simplicity of any passing, modish claims to dogmatic certainty. The diverse untameable otherness of the past provides a necessary check to any temptation to arrogance in the present.

These three expressions of powerful knowledge contain similarities around notions of time and chronology, people, behaviours/decision making and consequences of actions. School A identifies the importance of the broader chronological framework of historical events, knowing how one event is linked to another over time. In the literature, Kitson (2021) expresses the importance of using school history to help students explore the present and future. None of the teachers in this study seemed to mention that. In fact, School C made a point about going 'beyond' the preoccupations of our twenty-first-century lives, and their final point about arrogance in the present serves as a warning, perhaps, about the dangers of being influenced by the cultural values of the present when interpreting events of the past. Examples here might include using present-day attitudes towards LGBTQ+ rights to make moral judgements about laws (and attitudes) of the past which outlawed gay relationships rather than, perhaps, trying to understand the attitudes within their time. The importance of challenging sources of evidence, identified in the literature as procedural knowledge, is explored in School C in the idea of treating certainty 'with scepticism'.

School C's teachers offered the following vignette:

> Teaching which is research-led, dialogue-rich and grounded in independent research enables these disciplines to be nurtured. A lesson which, for instance, can embrace in discussion the intricacies of eleventh-century Byzantine court politics, theological debates surrounding the filioque clause, the impact of climate change on declining Muslim power in the Mediterranean and the architectural legacy of the Hagia Sophia helps finesse our understanding of the textured complexity of any human thinking and experience. It also offers a richly joyous imaginative journey.

This vignette unpicks a very specific part of a history course to illustrate the knowledge with which students might engage. The first sentence shows how important the 'research' of history becomes – that procedural knowledge of interpreting a range of sources. The teachers here also hint at pedagogy – how to teach – with 'dialogue-rich' classrooms and independent research becoming key classroom tools to help students engage. In the literature, Puustinen and Khawaja (2020) have explored what powerful pedagogies for school history might start to look like (although they have not used that specific term). This is an example of

Future 3 curriculum thinking, the idea of 'finessed' thinking and 'dialogue' suggests that the work of the history student here is never fully complete; there is never one true narrative of the past. The interpretation of architecture is a key type of procedural knowledge that the students are able to draw on to infer meaning, but the narrative of this region and its histories are not fully resolved until the students have engaged with a range of knowledge. It is worth noting too the place of climate change in this vignette. Changes to the climate are used to explain changing power relationships in this era; the substantive historical knowledge of Muslim power in the Mediterranean is still the focus of the lesson but climatic changes are one part of that narrative. In a curriculum that rushes towards Future 2 thinking, climate change could be a contemporary issue that teachers must engage students with, and under this thinking the climate becomes more significant than the historical narrative. This would be diminishing for students of history.

Based on these discussions, the ways in which school history can be considered powerful for young people could be expressed as follows:

? Deep, descriptive chronological knowledge of the past. This includes a knowledge of dates, locations, and people and their behaviours (individual, group and mass).

? Analysis of sources of historical data (such as contemporary narratives, physical evidence, architectural styles, written records and oral histories) to evidence and explain the past. Where the evidence allows this necessarily should be from a range of different perspectives to build up a holistic picture of the past (developing the skills of historiography or 'thinking historically').

? The propensity to place historical events into a broader framework of time, thus enabling our understanding of the causes and impacts of decisions that people have taken in the past.

Conclusions: towards humanities capabilities

The humanities subjects each take people as their central focus in some way. As such, the real educational power derives from what young people today can learn from the experiences of others. Developing Future 3 thinking across the humanities respects each of the subjects' individualities; history is different to geography and to RE (and to some of the other subjects not detailed here, such as classical civilisation). It also respects the substantive knowledge of the subjects, which has the potential to be vast. An overfocus on this can lead to rote learning facts and Future 1 thinking. Yet without knowledge of chronologies, deities or places, the subjects are devoid of any material through which students can make sense of what they are studying. The humanities also draw on a wide range of methodologies, such as narrative interpretation, which must be taught and practised so that students are able to make knowledge claims. The subjects are not seeking 'objective' truths in the same way that the sciences are, and nor are they seeking a personal response from the student in the ways that arts subjects might. The humanities are often victims of 'corruption', in which contemporary concerns like 'respect for one another' seem to become the main lesson aims. It is this that can tend towards Future 2 thinking.

The ways in which these subjects' powerful knowledges have been expressed here, based on the literature and real teachers' voices, could be a starting point for thinking about why the humanities really matter in schools. If this can be articulated well, then threats like the combining of humanities subjects and the shortening of Key Stage 3 (and therefore the loss of a year of study) can be challenged.

For discussion

For RE teachers:

? Is it right to show students controversial cartoons of the Prophet Muhammad? Would it make a difference if there were no Muslim students in the class?

? Which of the major world religions should be included in the curriculum? Which ones should be omitted (and why)? What role should humanism play?

? How important is considering the cultural makeup of your students when determining what should be taught?

For history teachers:

? To what extent should present-day perspectives influence the way in which the past is viewed?

? How important is it to make historical study 'relevant' to students today, and what does this relevance mean?

? How can history teaching move beyond the (possible) tokenism of Black History Month to enable a greater diversity of voices in the classroom?

For geography teachers:

? Is geography a humanity or a science subject, and does this categorisation matter?

? What should determine which places and processes are taught in the geography classroom?

? Should students be taught more about their local (everyday) environments so they can understand them in new ways, or more about distant places that they may never have heard of before?

Chapter 9

What might make the creative arts a powerful knowledge?

Humans have been creating works of art for as long as we have been on the planet. From cave paintings, traditional foods and dances to works of contemporary music and drama, the ways in which people make sense of their surroundings and themselves has always been a key component of human culture. The creative arts is a billion-dollar industry – including film, TV and music – but it also has a key role to play in the very essence of what it means to be a human: to think, to be, to do and to become as the world changes. As such, the arts have a close link to the idea of capabilities. Capabilities scholars would argue that for many cultures, access to, enjoyment of and participation in the arts would be a key human capability (e.g. Nussbaum, 2000). In their work on climate change education, a team of educationists led by Professor Nicola Walshe have developed the notion of 'ecocapabilities' (e.g. Walshe and Perry, 2022), which uses artistic expression to draw directly on the interface between science, geography and art, as a means to express and engage with the immediacy and challenge presented by the climate crisis.

Many young people engage with the work of contemporary artist Banksy. He is one of the most famous and celebrated artists of his generation; yet his true identity remains hidden, adding to his mysterious persona. As a street artist since the 1990s, his work is in the medium of graffiti, usually done by night in public places around the world, including Bristol, London and Jerusalem. One of his most iconic pieces is *Girl with Balloon*, which depicts a child drawn in black and white holding onto a piece of string attached to a vibrant red heart-shaped balloon floating above her. A 2017 survey by Samsung identified the work as the UK's number 1 favourite piece of art (as reported in *BBC News*, 2017). The work itself has been linked to various social and political campaigns. In 2014, Banksy painted a new version of the image to show his support for Syrian refugees as part of the #WithSyria campaign. He has always used art to remain relevant and to speak to his audience. In 2018, a framed version of the painting, created in 2006, was put up for sale at Sotheby's. It sold for a record-breaking £1 million, but as soon as the auction hammer fell the painting began slowly sinking into its frame where it was partly shredded, the cut pieces of the work appearing underneath to a room of shocked onlookers. Sotheby's later said that it was 'the first work in history ever created during a live auction' (quoted in Wolfe, n.d.). Banksy was behind the stunt; he had placed the work in the frame and given strict instructions to the auction house that it was not to be removed or it would ruin its artistic integrity. The stunt was meant to act as a symbolic protest against the futility of art and the commercialism and elitism of the art industry. His graffiti should be enjoyed by large numbers of people, not sold to the highest bidder and displayed privately. That was his intention. Ironically, the value of the piece increased and the new partially shredded work, now called *Love is in the Bin*, resold in October 2021 for £16 million (*BBC News*, 2021).

School art teachers have much inspiration to draw on from Banksy, especially as students seem to engage with his work more than that of artists in other, more traditional, mediums. Firstly, they can get students to imitate his style. This would involve using spray paints, picking locations (real or imagined) where art could go, and designing their compositions using simple shapes and iconic imagery. This deliberate practice develops the students' skills, such as the fine motor skills needed to control the deployment of paint on a surface. Yet there is much more of significant value that could be drawn from the study of Banksy's artwork. He is political. His art is designed to evoke a reaction in its audience. How the artist has used paint and the location of the work gives it significance and meaning. To understand Banksy, the art needs to be placed in its wider surroundings, which includes socio-political influences and the material 'lived experience'. The fact that Banksy creates new art from old is also something students could explore. This could be practically, in the form of reworking old pieces. We could also consider what this says both about those works, but also about art and the human spirit. Art has the ability to elicit feelings and reactions; students should be able to explore this to develop knowledge about art, knowledge of art and knowledge of themselves through art.

Students should also get the chance to experience the greatest artworks that humanity has created, either in the classroom or, better still, in a theatre, museum or gallery. Yet – as we saw in relation to English literature – there is a debate as to exactly what this canon of works should be and who gets to decide on their relative greatness. At best, a teacher would choose the pieces that are celebrated across a range of contexts, that have impacted history or changed the way in which we engage with each other in society, highlighting questions and opening up different ways of understanding the world. An example of a piece of art which does this might be Marcel Duchamp's *Fountain*. Some of these artworks might be selected by the students themselves according to what matters to them. At worst, these choices can lead to accusations of presenting a particular view of the world or causing offence. Art should provoke, but getting the balance right between provocative and offensive is a challenge.

The creative arts can include a range of subjects and this chapter includes art, drama, music and design technology (DT). DT is one of those subjects that does not fit with the others quite so well as it has a greater mathematical and scientific application. However, as there is a creative process involved it is included in this chapter.

The arts should form a central role in the school curriculum, yet time given over to the arts has been declining. Opportunities to take part in whole-school productions, art workshops and extracurricular activities outside the taught curriculum have reduced, especially as art, music and drama are not part of the more coveted STEM group of subjects. DT would be covered by 'technology', and some attempts have been made to shoehorn art in to form STEAM subjects. The acronym has had some success, but without any real curricular attempt to realise the value of art in the curriculum and beyond. Creative arts were not included in the EBacc and as such their status has reduced in state schools. The arts are in danger of becoming the preserve of private schools.

Creative art knowledge in schools

The arts seems to have become a victim in the perceived push for a knowledge-rich curriculum to the extent that Simon Toyne (2021), in his chapter in *What Should Schools Teach?*, describes music education as being in 'crisis'. Drama teacher and education writer Martin Robinson (2021: 89) explains it as follows:

> A school that shrinks the arts provision that its pupils can access is making a decision about what they think their priorities should be. If they are guided by utilitarian choices then it is easy for them to cut back on arts programmes ... But if they are guided by the desire to educate their pupils as to what is important to them as human beings to make sense of the world and their place within it, then they will do their very best to ensure the arts have a proper and sustainable place in their curriculum.

There is a battle of ideologies here. In a knowledge-rich curriculum, the utilitarian need to get good grades in a variety of subjects seems to trump child-centred perceptions of helping students to explore themselves and their place in the world. Yet to dismiss the arts simply as a form of child-centred ideology neglects the knowledge that the study of the arts is able to impart.

Art educationists have long had a challenge when it comes to discussing 'knowledge'. This problem is mirrored in the art world, and in the academic discipline which discusses and supports its work. The renowned art educationist Elliot Eisner (2008: 2) asserts that 'no one knows what knowledge goes into art, or what knowledge comes out of it'. Part of the challenge, he continues, is the notion that the discipline of art as researched and taught throughout the world lacks any form of central coherence:

> The major art schools ... know one another ... because they are part of the international circuit of the art market. But there is no place to go to find out how art is taught in provincial China, India, or South America. (Eisner, 2008: 3)

As part of his own research, (Eisner 2008: 4) interviewed a series of artists and found many who felt there is no 'knowledge' at all in art:

> One said that artists know nothing, and that's why they make art. Another said that there is no difference between artists and others because we all work for the same 'entertainment industry'. And my

> favourite cynic wrote that artists only think they have knowledge,
> but really they just use their brains 'in a strange way'.

....

James Elkins' 2001 book was even entitled *Why Art Cannot Be Taught*, suggesting that art has a deeper and more ethereal quality than can be captured and packaged in a neat way for students. Art could be seen more as a way of thinking and approaching the world, as Frances Whitehead perhaps rather flippantly said in recorded conversation: 'artists do not think outside the box: there is no box' (quoted in Elkins, 2001: 47).

Ruth Ashbee (2021: 91), in her work discussing art in schools, argues that the subject 'tends to be conceived of as a practical subject with the quest embodied in creative products'. Similar conversations also exist in music education: 'where art deals in light, music deals in sound; colours are in many ways analogous to notes; composition is key to both' (Ashbee, 2021: 94). In drama it is the ways in which an actor creates feelings and emotions through their actions, taking the words from the playwright and bringing them to life, and in DT it is the process of designing and making a piece of technology that is central. The creative work of composition and performance is at the heart of the creative arts subjects, yet to achieve this requires procedural knowledge.

Creative arts as procedural knowledge

Procedural knowledge – or being skilled at creating pieces of art – such as playing music or painting, is often how the subjects are conceived in schools. Students practise the creative art of developing and refining a piece of work under the watchful eye of a teacher. As Dido Powell (2021: 76) identifies in *What Should Schools Teach?*, procedural knowledge is 'how to make an artwork; the sequential application of practical skills, involving hand, eye and brain co-ordination; an ability to follow instructions; and powers of selection or judgement'. The procedural knowledge of art would include the skilful ways in which artists work to sculpt, to paint or to create 'art'. The ability to really 'see' would count as key procedural knowledge, as well as having the manual dexterity to transfer that in some way to paper or create it as a sculpture or other form of artistic expression.

In music the procedural knowledge involves practising instruments to make sounds, and knowing how to do this to evoke emotion. It also includes performance, both individually and in groups. With this type of knowledge, practice is the key to success. According to research, it takes about two and a half years to reach Grade 1 in an instrument, with each additional grade taking another year (Toyne, 2021), assuming daily practice and weekly lessons. In DT, the procedural knowledge involves knowing how to use computer-aided design (CAD) software and the practical techniques of using different materials to build finished products. Yet the arts subjects rely on the substantive knowledge of the professional worlds and their various academic disciplines, including fine art, art history, drama, theatre studies and engineering.

Creative arts as substantive knowledge

The last section argued that the creative arts subjects involve developing students' procedural knowledge, so they are able to create art that evokes (or provokes) a reaction of some kind in its audience. That makes identifying any sort of discernible substantive knowledge of the arts, some form of content to learn, more challenging. Despite this, a number of writers have proposed lists of possible substantive knowledge. For first year undergraduate art students, James Elkins (2012: 67) suggests 'colour theory, composition, lectures on space, time, and form, texture, movement, identity theory'. These ideas might start to express a form of substantive knowledge of the subject. He goes on to argue:

. . . .

Art can provide knowledge in uninteresting ways – by showing us the Franco-Prussian war, by recording the fashions of fifteenth-century Florence – but if it provides knowledge in a more interesting way, that knowledge has to somehow be intrinsic to the artwork itself. (Elkins, 2012: 39)

. . . .

Ruth Ashbee (2021) identifies perspective, anatomy, looking and noticing, and colour theory as part of the substantive knowledge of art.

Art history provides an important source of substantive knowledge, although it is a way of seeing art in its own right. How the great works of art were created, and the movements they drew from and inspired, is an

important aspect to teach students in schools. As Ashbee (2021: 92) argues:

> knowledge of art history can inform and inspire students' practical work, which in turn allows greater appreciation of the work of artists over time, since students have practically participated in this 'great conversation' in their own drawing and painting.

A focus on art history in the classroom might see students studying cubism, surrealism, modernism or postmodernism, amongst many more, and using this to create their own artwork.

Despite this grand ambition for school art, Mary Myatt (2021: 152) warns that 'whilst there is much creative work of great quality produced by pupils in school, there appears to be less focus on the explicit teaching of artists and their traditions'. For her, there is a greater emphasis on students creating their own work than studying others'. As a result, she offers a harsh critique of the state of art knowledge in schools, which has been echoed by other writers. As Powell (2021: 74) has observed:

> Pupils, as part of their [GCSE] exam, are required to show evidence of research into a well-known artist's works … This investigation is, however, unsupported by a programme of art history teaching; consequently, pupils tend to present brief biographies on artists accompanied by painted or drawn copies of enlarged fragments of artworks in a formulaic manner … It is an approach that removes the quoted artist's work from its artistic context, especially the relevance of stylistic techniques, and imposes a prescribed narrow framework for pupils' visual expression.

For Powell, the demands of the examination seek to separate the practical act of creating a piece of original artwork from a deeper understanding of the various art movements that inspired that piece of work. According to the critique from Powell and Myatt, students are missing out on the ways in which art might be considered powerful in a push to produce something tangible for a set of examiners.

In drama, substantive knowledge includes reading, watching and performing the greatest plays ever written. This includes the various forms of theatre and performance that have inspired those works, from Greek theatre, dance, musical theatre, and movements like *commedia dell'arte* and surreal theatre. Knowledge includes where these art forms come from, what they set out to achieve in terms of evoking a reaction from an audience, and examples of the work.

In music, substantive knowledge includes the great musical works of human creation, the study of which can be split into theory, analysis and composition, all of which requires knowledge. Ideas such as style, genre, pitch, timbre, melody, harmony, beats, bars, and more make up the specific areas of study in school music.

In DT, the substantive knowledge involves a complete cycle of designing, making and producing a product, so this requires knowledge of materials, tools and techniques, and the costs and sustainability of each; technical knowledge – for example, of gears, pulleys and electronics; and knowledge of design, such as symmetry and form. There is also a need to understand great technological innovations over time and their significance in the world of engineering (Ashbee, 2021).

Knowledge of the great works of art are often used as a proxy measure of cultural literacy. If this is missing from the curriculum in a push for students to generate their own creative pieces, with a tokenistic nod to well-known artworks, then students will not develop that deeper culturally significant understanding. Thus, knowledge of art history, and the ways in which great pieces of art have influenced culture, is an expression of how art can be a powerful knowledge for young people.

Creative arts as powerful knowledge

As school subjects, the arts are clearly not on some epistemological search for objective truths, unlike science, which holds a much more central role in the curriculum. There are facts to learn, drawn from the substantive knowledge of the different art forms, and a focus on learning these by rote at the expense of exploring creativity would create a Future 1 curriculum. Yet using the arts to explore generic themes like 'gangs', 'bullying' or 'drugs' is Future 2 curriculum thinking. Martin Robinson (2021: 91) discusses this in relation to drama lessons: 'Such methods and techniques had little to do with the "art of theatre" but everything to do with enabling children to express their feelings and opinions within a restricted frame of reference.'

This is an example of curriculum 'corruption'; students are not learning about great works of art or pieces of drama, but instead are being asked to engage with generic competencies. Great works of art, of course, can tackle difficult subjects and enable students to engage with complex and challenging ideas, if taught well, and this is at the heart of Future 3 thinking. John Dewey, writing in 1934, argued that whilst science states meaning, art 'expresses' it. Thus, art is more about representations of truth than universal claims to it.

The empowering nature of art comes through its epistemological base; knowledge in arts is co-constructed between the creators who design the art in the first place, the artists/musicians/actors/designers who create or perform the art, and the audience who views or listens or observes and interacts with that art. The audience therefore plays a central role in the construction of meaning. In this sense it can be seen as a form of 'embodied' knowledge, or 'embodied art reflection' (Bube, 2021), as the observer has an immediate reaction which can be explored. This is a type of knowledge which is dynamic, relational and always changing. As Shogo Tanaka (2011: 149) articulates, it is a knowledge, 'which is not distinctly explicit, conscious, mentally representative, or articulated. It is, however, well known by the body or through the body, when it is practiced.'

This notion of knowledge being 'embodied' takes us beyond simple explorations of substantive and procedural knowledge, important though they are, to something much more personal and powerful for a young person. A skilled artist knows how to create a piece of art that elicits a response in those who consume it. Whether that is a painting, piece of music or performance, the ability to produce a response can enable the artist to play with emotion and feeling. Suanna Langer (1957: 6) argues that art can evoke a form of 'feeling'. Simon Toyne (2021: 109) praises music for its ability to 'tap into our psyche and engage, soothe, nourish, excite, invigorate, upset, challenge and change us'. The arts are empowering for young people due to their ability to provoke an emotional response of some kind; the study of art in schools enables students to explore and respond to this in some way.

Teacher voice

Art

Table 9.1: Results of art teacher workshop

School A	School B	School C
Opportunity to express themselves through a creative outlet. To be able to openly interpret and discuss art in all its forms; you learn to express opinions and articulate thoughts and feelings. Formal elements of art such as line, colour, form, texture. Everyone can have surface appreciation of art but looking at the use of colour to convey emotion is magic.	Understand and use a visual language. Communicate conceptual thoughts and ideas. Appreciation for historical and contemporary art and culture. Engage and change the way you look at the world around you.	Art is a reflection of life – therefore it is about everything and reflects every subject area. Art is a cross-curricular subject, most notably in the element of analysis. The development of technical skills and techniques – the tools with which to express ideas, information and feelings through creative activity in the visual arts.

Teachers from School C offer a vignette:

. . . .

We are looking at objects in surrealist art with Year 9, so this enables us to make connections with other subjects. For example, history: surrealism as a concept is a product of the time in which it was first conceived; it is derived from dadaism, a reaction to the horrors of the First World War. Psychology/science: surrealists were inspired by the psychoanalysis of Sigmund Freud and new discoveries about how the brain works.

Surrealism uses a range of techniques from traditional painting skills to create an illusion of 'reality', to automatism which deploys accident and the element of chance. This challenges our notion of skill, enabling us to value risk-taking as part of the creative process, which encourages us to look at the world in new and interesting ways, not to take what we see at face value. The impact of surrealism has been total – we cannot imagine a visual world today without it. Students are encouraged to look around them for examples in film, on TV, online, in advertising, alongside others. The topic stimulates their imagination and encourages expressive and individual approaches. This is our 'unique and powerful knowledge', but we do not see that this needs to be any different from any other subject. The overall approach – making connections with other subjects as well as with other aspects of life, both contemporary and historical – can and should be part of any vibrant curriculum.

. . . .

The expressions of powerful knowledge identified here by the three groups of art teachers broadly follow the types of knowledge as discussed in some of the key texts by curriculum theorists. The first expression of knowledge they identify is a type of substantive knowledge – the notion of the context of an artwork and some of the specificities of the subject, like colour, form and texture. The second point is much more akin to procedural knowledge – the 'skills and techniques' needed to create art. All three sets of teachers discuss the importance of students being able to express themselves and use art as a creative outlet for their own emotions. This ties in with the literature, which says that meaning in art is 'embodied' – co-constructed with those who observe the art; the artist puts their emotions into a piece which can then be experienced and interpreted by the audience.

The teachers in School C are keen to present the subject in cross-curricular terms, identifying that art has links with lots of other subjects, and this theme continues into their vignette. The vignette discusses the ways in which a topic on surrealism in Year 9 could be powerful for young people. Mary Myatt (2021) and Ruth Ashbee (2021) both argue that teachers put more emphasis on the creation of the art by the students, driven by the demands of the examination, rather than deep exploration of the context in which art is created or the emotions that it is designed to evoke. The teachers in this study do not follow this trend; they have begun to explore the value of art beyond the technical ability to create it and to place surrealism into a wider context. Yet these teachers have expressed value in terms of cross-curricular links rather than anything intrinsic in the artwork itself. The teachers here seem more interested in looking at surrealist art through other subjects. They even argue that the powerful knowledge of art does not need 'to be any different to any other subject'.

This book is arguing against that position. Art does have a unique role to play in the curriculum. There is surrealist poetry and surrealist histories, but what the powerful knowledge of art can express is how studying art can help a student to understand surrealism, and why this might be important. This was perhaps under-expressed in the teacher responses.

Despite this, the vignette does illustrate why art can be considered powerful. If we look beyond the attempts to link the topic to other school subjects, we can focus on the discussion of a particular art movement: surrealism. Its proponents were creating artwork in particular social and political contexts, and their work evokes strong reactions that young people can explore in the classroom. This is not about studying other subjects but seeing how the composition of specific works in a given genre provokes a reaction and what the interpretation of this means for young people. It is the deep exploration of these artworks and the meanings that derive from this that could claim to be powerful for young people.

Drama

Table 9.2: Results of drama teacher workshop

School A	School B	School C
Knowledge of social, cultural, historical and political aspects of theatre and the human condition. Theoretical and practical application of key concepts in historical and contemporary theatre.	Theoretical and practical procedures that explore culture, society and texts, and how they are seen and reflected through a performance.	Detailed understanding of a diverse range of drama, dramatic forms/genres and theatre history, and its place in a social, cultural, historical and political context.

School A	School B	School C
The ability to engage, explore, empathise and challenge perceptions of the human condition.	Critically reading our world in a way that transcends text and vocal communication and can both connect and polarise people and audiences.	Knowledge and experience that will permit creative responses to stimuli or play texts to inform interpretive decisions and convey relevant messages to key target audiences. Development of students' levels of empathy – to use drama as a means to 'put themselves in another's shoes'.

There is a remarkable consistency in the first expression of the powerful knowledge of drama across the teachers in the three case study schools. They all write about the ability to explore social, cultural and political ideas. There is a danger that this translates into a Future 2 curriculum, as illustrated in the literature, but this is not the case: School A is keen to ensure that this knowledge is about 'aspects of theatre' rather than simply acts of self, and School C identifies 'dramatic forms/genres'. It is clear here that drama is driving the knowledge and not simply a vehicle for expressing a wider range of generic values. The teachers also identify meaning as being socially constructed between the actor/director/ writer and the audience; they mention emotions and perceptions connecting and polarising audiences as a deliberate practice. This is where School C's point about empathy arises; creating a piece of drama to evoke an empathetic response from an audience requires deep understanding of the emotion, how to provoke it and how to lead an audience.

School C offered the following curriculum vignette:

. . . .

Year 12 and Year 13 students are expected to study the text of Aristophanes' Lysistrata, written and first performed in Athens in 411 BC. But with what aim in mind? They are required to take the text and think like a twenty-first-century director, performing this

2,500-year-old text for a modern-day audience. The primary task is to come up with a detailed plan for the reinterpretation of the text so that it is accessible to an audience and can convey a relevant message to them. The original play was an anti-war polemic and certainly it could be used as such today, but the Peloponnesian War would need to be rebranded as a conflict (perhaps in its widest sense) that resonates today. The fact that in the original play a group of women are attempting to bring about social change (something risible at the time) might offer possibilities in a feminist/equality arena. Students must have a detailed understanding of the original performance conditions so that their proposals can be informed by its first outing. They must apply the techniques of a key theatre practitioner who has had a significant effect on theatre practice in the past and, through their proposals, seek to bring about their own degree of social change. Thus, by developing their own imaginative responses to a creative brief, they must have a clear understanding of theatrical possibilities, seek to comment on a key current cultural or political issue, and apply the practices of the recent and not so recent past to give power to their ability to communicate cogently to an audience of their own design.

. . . .

This vignette illustrates how the knowledge of drama can be empowering for students. The substantive knowledge that students gain is the socio-political setting of the play, imbued with politics, feminism and war themes, but the students are being asked to reset this in a contemporary context, which requires another layer of substantive knowledge. Furthermore, a knowledge of drama techniques is required to bring these themes to the stage. These themes are not ends in themselves (which might evoke a Future 2 curriculum) but feature in an existing text. Thought also needs to go into the procedural knowledge of performance, drawing on dramatic styles and techniques and how to elicit the desired reaction from an audience.

Music

Table 9.3: Results of music teacher workshop

School A	School B	School C
Rigorous understanding of a range of academic skills in theory, analysis and instrumental performance skill. Creative response through performance, composition and listening activities. The increasing knowledge of how to work with a range of different people and skill levels towards a cohesive common goal.	Improving students' listening skills and analysis so they can make sense of what they hear. Allowing students to perform in front of their peers to grow in confidence. Developing fine motor skills and dexterity by playing instruments. Being more globally aware by studying traditional music from around the world.	An aural and practical knowledge and application of musical elements (particularly rhythm, pitch, harmony) because of their application to the different disciplines of performance, composition and listening. An in-depth understanding of these elements makes possible not only the observation and appreciation of art (music), but the shared participation in it too.

The teachers here all identify different ways in which music knowledge is significant for young people. A similarity in their responses is in the identification of the substantive knowledge of music theory. School C teachers give examples of rhythm, pitch and harmony, as well as suggest that 'composition' and 'performance' are empowering. Surprisingly, the teachers from School B are the only ones to identify the significance of traditional music engendering global knowledge, yet this was picked up in the literature as being a significant element of music education. They also identify the significance of 'listening' as key procedural knowledge. How to listen, critically, is something that music teachers can teach, and School B identifies how this can lead to creative responses. The notion of shared participation and teamwork is also significant; although, of course, the arts are not the only subjects where this occurs.

School C offered this vignette:

. . . .

Students study elements (musical and otherwise) of Handel's *Messiah* at A level, including historical and social context, perform- ing forces, its historical and musical influences and influence, rhythm, pitch, harmony, instrumentation, texture and word-setting. This knowledge gives students the ability to perform the work with appropriate style, to compose in that style (and others) using those musical features, and to aurally identify those features in other pieces of music.

. . . .

This vignette picks out many of the features of music study that were explored in the expression of powerful knowledge – placing it into its his- torical and musical setting, the specifics of rhythm and pitch, and the significance of listening and identifying features. The performance ele- ment, requiring procedural knowledge of instruments, is also identifiable.

DT

Table 9.4: Results of DT teacher workshop

School A	School B	School C
Real-world problems like the climate crisis, ocean pollution and renewable energy need practical, creative solutions. Knowledge of the iterative design process of develop, test and evaluate.	Practical skills – computer-aided design (CAD)/ computer-aided manufacture (CAM) skills. Knowledge of materials and their properties.	The core concepts of making things – for example, cutting materials. (Accuracy is the same whether it is a garden shed, a particle accelerator or a fusion reactor!) Cross-curricular links to material science in areas like medical robotics.

School A	School B	School C
Knowledge of sustainable and responsible design develops empathy.	Knowledge of the sustainability of materials, especially regarding environmental issues. Developing fine motor skills, especially through soldering and sketching.	Looking at the needs of individuals across all of society, both on an individual level and as a wider user group. Aiding individuals – for example, helping those with disabilities (deafness, colour blindness, and so forth) to function better in our existing society. Knowledge of wider environmental issues associated with making. Learning traditional skills like silversmithing.

The three groups of DT teachers all focus on slightly different elements of DT education. School A links DT to technological solutions to global issues to give the subject real-world, contemporary relevance, something not picked up by the other schools. School C seems very keen to link DT to other areas of the curriculum rather than focusing on what makes the subject unique. They were also the only teachers to pick up on traditional skills, here mentioning silversmithing.

What they all do agree on is the idea of making and producing something, and they all identify a core set of specific skills, such as the use of CAD, which relies on the procedural knowledge of DT. The environment seems to be a key idea for all three sets of teachers, with the environmental sustainability of materials being a core theme.

School C offered this vignette:

. . . .

Students choose their own direction from a very open list of options for their GCSE piece. They, as individuals, steer the project guided by their own thoughts, ideas and values. They follow a structure to document their progress, but must decide within that how their time will be spent and which resources and approaches to problem solving they will use. They choose outside advisors or clients to design for and listen to their input to help guide their projects. They make their own progress throughout and, in the end, with help from their advisor, evaluate the outcome and identify possible improvements. The entire project can give an outstanding sense of achievement and many students comment on how positive the challenge has been.

. . . .

The teachers here have identified the process of DT project work, similar to the planning-making-evaluating cycle identified in the literature, but have not really exemplified the knowledge required to bring the projects to fruition. The teachers talk about the importance of independent learning, which is a key feature of project work, but independent learning is not done in isolation. DT teachers are part of this process, helping to advise and teach specific elements of the work. A DT project that works on, for example, a new design to help a disabled person will require a range of background knowledge to place the project in its cultural setting. Students engaging in this project would research this knowledge as part of their work.

Conclusions: towards creative arts capabilities

Based on the discussions here, the powerful knowledge of the creative arts subjects could be expressed in the following ways:

? Knowledge of the socio-cultural and political settings in which art is created and how this has influenced the nature of the art, and how the art itself has influenced the culture around it. This should be exemplified by exposure to great works of art from the past and present from around the world.

？ Knowledge of how art is able to evoke and provoke a reaction from those who create it and how that creates meaning with those who interact with it through embodied knowledge. In art this is through the careful use of colour, texture and tone; in drama through ideas like style and communication; in music through key and melody; and in DT through functionality and aesthetics.

？ Knowledge of how to create art in different styles and genres. The procedural knowledge here is followed by deliberate practice to develop skill over extended periods of time.

？ Knowledge of art across time and space. This would include traditional art, music and drama from different cultures around the world and how these interact to create new hybrid forms. In DT this could include traditional skills like silversmithing.

The creative arts play an important role in the curriculum, but the challenge school art teachers face is to recognise and vocalise exactly what this role is. The practical ability to create works of art is a recognised part of the subject, but there appears to be less of a consensus amongst the teachers in this study, and those reported elsewhere (e.g. Myatt, 2018), about the significance of the arts in the broader socio-cultural context or the power of interpretation to infer meaning. Art GCSE courses seem to lack this too, preferring to focus on the creation of art, with a tokenistic nod to the origins of the style. By framing the debate around the notions of embodied and powerful knowledges, teachers can begin to articulate why the arts matter so much in the school curriculum, and therefore how art contributes to students' capabilities to think in new ways about the world, to go beyond the everyday, to be inspired and actively engaged in conversations about our culture. It is this that develops students' cultural capital. Framed in this way, arts teachers can articulate why due time and curriculum space needs to be given over to their subjects.

For discussion

？ Which pieces of art/drama/music/technology would you choose to expose your students to, and why? Who should make the decision about relevance?

？ How important is the academic, university-based world of the creative arts disciplines to teachers of creative arts subjects in schools?

? If great art should provoke a reaction, should it offend?

? Should DT even be considered an arts subject? Does this matter?

Chapter 10

What might make languages a powerful knowledge?

Those of us who promote subjects as the heart of the school curriculum can learn a lot from Latin. The classical language was once regarded as the ultimate academic subject – the symbol of an educated person. It was a compulsory component of a grammar school education, and from Victorian times right through to the 1950s the content and methods of the subject changed very little. Latin teachers would introduce students to vocabulary and grammar and engage them in translations of ancient texts. As students advanced, the wonders of the ancient world were available for them to enjoy in the original language, such as the *Iliad* telling the epic tale of the Trojan War. Yet by the late 1980s, Latin had all but disappeared in schools, preserved mainly in academically selective independent spheres. Its decline tells us that no subject can ever claim to be a central tenet of a school curriculum.

Ian McMillan (2016) has studied the changing fortunes of Latin. As he argues, Latin was the preserve of the elite. Perceived to be the gateway subject to prestigious universities and the professions, mastery of Latin was a prerequisite for many advanced courses; Oxford and Cambridge universities only dropped it as a requirement in 1960 (McMillan, 2016: 26). Students in secondary modern schools did not study the subject at all; it was deemed too difficult, too academic and not practical enough. When the comprehensive school system was introduced, many of the former grammar schools dropped Latin from their curriculum. By the 1960s, the decline in Latin teaching in schools had begun. By the time the national curriculum for England and Wales was introduced in the late 1980s, Latin was not part of the compulsory diet of subjects that would form part of every young person's education.

There are many reasons why Latin, as one of the Classics subjects (with ancient Greek), did not prosper through these educational changes. These are partly cultural. As John Sharwood Smith (1977: 2) argues, 'The institutionalised pre-eminence of Classics played some part in keeping the upper classes on top.' In the era of comprehensivisation of education and arguments about equality of access, Latin – with its elitist pretensions – was not a welcome addition. Science became much more of a marker of an educated person than a knowledge of the Classics, bolstered by the pre-eminence of science within the school system. There was no longer any need to study Latin. The introduction of 'classical civilisation', effectively a humanities subject that initiated students to the classical word of ancient Greece and Rome, was an attempt to broaden the appeal of the subject and to keep Latin alive in schools in some form. Latin lost its prestige, and as such the number of students opting to study it plummeted. Currently, fewer than 2% of state schools offer Latin, compared to 49% of independent schools (Collen, 2023: 22).

A further reason why Latin failed to prosper, according to Martin Forrest (1996) was due to its teachers' stubborn refusal to change. Latin had a set methodology: a rigorous focus on translation and grammar exercises. It also has what McMillan (2016: 25) describes as high 'cultural surrender' value, meaning that the educational benefits of Latin only really arise once the subject has been studied for a long period of time; there are no quick wins. There was a fear that any attempt to 'dumb down' the subject could mean a loss of its academic integrity. As McMillan (2016: 30) continues, 'The reason that multiple crises impacted upon Latin teaching was that warning signals such as calls for new methodology or improved cultural surrender value were ignored.'

In part, teachers of Latin failed to argue the case effectively for the educational benefits of studying the subject. They had not explained how and why Latin can offer young people powerful knowledge. Had that been articulated clearly at the time, then there could have been a much stronger case for the continued inclusion of Latin in the school curriculum.

All is not lost in the story of Latin in schools. In recent years, there has been a renewed push for its inclusion, in part inspired by TV presenters like Professor Mary Beard, but also due to a realisation of the benefits that come from studying ancient languages. September 2022 saw the start of a four-year, £4-million scheme, funded by the Department for Education, to reintroduce Latin to forty state schools with an aim to increase the number of students sitting Latin GCSE (Bryant, 2021). As part of this, the lyrics of Taylor Swift's 'Bad Blood' have been translated into Latin by Cambridge researchers in an attempt to make the subject more interesting to young people (Weale, 2022).

Language education in schools

The opportunity for students to learn to communicate in a language that is not their native tongue has been a key component of education systems around the world. Broadly speaking, languages can be subdivided into the classical languages of ancient Greek and Latin and modern foreign languages (MFL), which includes the languages actively spoken around the world today.

If the story of Latin is one of terminal curricular decline, then the story of MFL is a more mixed picture. Studying a language has been part of the EBacc since 2010, but despite this there has been a 30–50% drop in the numbers of students sitting an MFL GCSE in the UK since 2013 (according to a BBC report by Jeffreys, 2019). The languages studied has changed over time too. French and German have seen the biggest declines – since 2002 the number of French GCSE entries has dropped by 51% and German by 64%; in three local authorities there were no entries at all for GCSE German in 2017. There has been an increase in the number of students choosing Spanish (of 49% since 2002) and Mandarin (Chinese) (Jeffreys, 2019). In Wales, all students are required to study the Welsh language either as a main or second language until the age of 16 and this accounts for recent rises in uptake. So, the nature of language education is changing and, as is the case for the classical languages, it seems that independent schools have the largest number of entries for MFL courses. There are likely many factors to explain this, but whilst languages tend to be optional in most schools (despite the demands of the EBacc), many independent schools still ensure that students take at least one language to GCSE (Collen, 2023: 26).

The changing fortunes of various languages in the curriculum can be explained by a variety of reasons. These not only determine which languages are to be studied, but also how they are taught. The most popular languages in the world as measured by number of speakers (not necessarily native users) are English, Mandarin Chinese, Hindi, Spanish, French and then Arabic (Dyvik, 2023), but this does not seem to account for the choices of languages in UK schools; Arabic and Hindi are not widely taught.

At the heart of languages education is an ideological battle between those who see it as a means to introduce cultural understanding of people and places and those who see it as a means to enhance economic potential. In the middle of the last century, a key motivation came from the desire to introduce young people to certain cultures and lifestyles from around the world, hence teaching those chosen languages. Writing about languages education for American youth in 1948, Nicholas Murray Butler (1948: v) stated:

the ability to speak and read with ease at least one foreign language is more than ever necessary if the mind and imagination of American youth are to be set free for expansion beyond the narrow horizon of vocational interests and national prejudice.

According to this view, languages education plays a key role beyond simply learning how to speak and write; it evokes cultural understanding which takes young people beyond their narrow, known world. This approach comes from a child-centred ideology. As Mercer (1950: 118) suggests, 'Thus, the student learns something of the geography and the economic, political and social institutions of the country at the same time he is acquiring a vocabulary.'

Pedagogically, this approach to languages education would involve learning about the country (or countries) where the language is spoken; mapping its geography; and learning abouts its customs, food, clothing and religious beliefs. Learning the vocabulary and grammar would provide a means through which to introduce these ideas.

More recently, there has been a much more utilitarian intent for languages education, linked to the changing needs of international business. French, German and Spanish are traditionally studied in UK schools as these countries are key trading partners. When the UK joined the European Economic Community in 1973, language education played an important role in preparing people for the new international workplace.

Yet global business has changed. Despite English being the international language of business, the modern workforce is much more globalised, hence the renewed interest in languages from around the world. In 2000, Jim O'Neill from the bank Goldman Sachs predicted the four countries that would be the biggest economies in the world by 2050, dubbing them the BRIC(S): Brazil (Portuguese speaking), Russia, India and China (with

South Africa added in 2015). He went on to identify the next wave of global economic giants, following on from the BRICS – the MINT countries: Mexico, Indonesia, Nigeria and Taiwan (e.g. Tett, 2010). It is the interest in these countries that has resulted in the rise in languages like Mandarin and, alongside Brexit changing the UK's trading relationship with Europe, led to a reduction in the more traditional school subjects of French and German.

Pedagogically, this version of languages education focuses mainly on learning vocabulary and grammar and acquiring the ability to speak, write, read and listen to it, and as such it can be stripped of cultural content about the people and places where it is spoken. Shirley Lawes (2007: 92), in her contribution to *The Corruption of the Curriculum*, has argued that this transition has changed MFL subjects for the worse. As she explains:

. . . .

the view of policy makers of the place and value of foreign languages learning in our education system is that is a functional skill with an assumed practical purpose relevant to business needs or future employment.

. . . .

She is even more sceptical of the supposed vocational purpose of languages education as a reason to study a chosen language. Part of the reason for the decline of MFL in schools is, according to Lawes this false idea of the link between languages and better paid jobs. As she argues, 'Young people were never fooled by the idea that "you'll get a better job if you speak a language" and they are unlikely to now, given the dominance of English as a world language' (Lawes, 2007: 92–93).

The switch to comprehensive education also coincided with an increase in the accessibility of international travel and paid holidays for workers. Suddenly, all young people were able to travel to other countries cheaply, which created another need for language education. The impact of this, however, was another form of 'corruption' of the curriculum, as Lawes (2007: 89) goes on to explain:

. . . .

the emphasis on the functional use of language in practical situations paved the way for an emptying out of any serious linguistic or cultural content in favour of what was to become little more than a survival toolkit for a holiday abroad.

. . . .

Recently, there have been calls to reintroduce specific languages back into schools. The focus is mostly on indigenous languages that have been lost over time in the great push towards modernity; these lost languages provide a tangible link back to the cultural heritage of places. As Wade Davis (2009: 3) has eloquently argued, language is 'an old growth forest of the mind', storing past ways of being, understandings of landscape and the uniqueness of people. Studies from Usborne et al. (2011) aimed at teaching modern Canadian children the languages spoken by the indigenous peoples as a means to help them to connect with their nation's heritage. Welsh is a part of the school curriculum in Wales, although the amount of Welsh language education varies by school (SSCE Cymru, n.d.). This process is also deeply political in an era of increased nationalism, especially as the students may not be directly descended from those who traditionally spoke the languages. Teaching children to speak the traditional national language of the place where they live can help to evoke images of the past and provide a tangible link to their nation.

There are, of course, practical considerations regarding which languages are selected for inclusion in a school's offering. The availability of teachers who speak those languages and can teach them to a high enough standard could be limited. Primary schools experience the challenge of providing specialist language teaching. As Mary Myatt (2021: 179) argues, 'language expertise is not the reality for most [primary] schools'. Thus, change happens slowly, and if student numbers are reducing in some languages, it is not straightforward to simply swap out one language for another; a new teacher with different expertise would probably be required.

Knowledge in language education

Modern languages have been described as a 'quasi-natural phenomena' (Ashbee, 2021: 87), meaning that although they are created and maintained by people, there is a sense that they evolve naturally over time. New words are introduced, older ones fade into obscurity and there is no central control over this process; it happens with the evolution of culture over time. Oxford University Press (Nanji, 2023) identified 'rizz' as its word of the year 2023.[1] The English language is evolving not just in the UK, but also as a result of the many people who speak it as a second (or other) language around the world; 'World Englishes' is a recognised field of linguistic study (e.g. Schneider, 2020). As a result, as Lawes (2021: 132) has claimed, 'knowledge that constitutes the discipline of foreign languages has become "a moveable feast" and is disputed.'

Language knowledge can be both vertically and horizontally structured, according to Bernstein's (2000) categorisation. The language itself relies on progression over time and as such could be described as having a vertical knowledge structure. Students need to learn vocabulary, and then be able to use grammar to make it make sense. Rote learning of key phrases can enable a back-and-forth conversation, but, for progression, verb conjugations, word endings and various gender agreements need to be understood. The present tense is usually studied first, and basic conversational skills developed before more complex grammar and specific vocabulary is introduced. Different tenses can then be introduced. Once mastered, students can begin to translate texts into and from the target language. This requires time and patience and builds up over the years of schooling, ideally involving immersion in the language through conversations with native speakers or visits to countries where the language is spoken.

Yet within language education there is an element of horizontal knowledge structure if the more cultural elements of the countries where the language is spoken are being studied. Topics like clothes, food, customs and locations can be studied in any order and returned to at a greater level of linguistic detail, so this requires teachers to make a decision around the sequencing of topics and ideas.

The substantive knowledge of languages includes the various rules of the language: its long list of vocabulary (which itself evolves and changes over time), verb conjugations and grammar. For classical languages this helps with translations into and out of the target language. For modern languages the substantive knowledge would also include the spoken elements, the correct pronunciation of words and the sounds of the language. It includes knowledge of the places where the language is spoken, including its people, customs, clothing and food. It is this cultural element that Shirley Lawes (2007; 2021) claims has been lost in a push towards a vocational ideology. This knowledge is substantive: there are

---

1   'Rizz' is a term for attractiveness or charm, believed to have derived from 'charisma'. To 'rizz up' is to chat someone up. It began as a slang term on social media and is mainly used by young people!

things that can be learnt, including dates of key historical events and national holidays and recipes for national dishes. At higher levels students are encouraged to discuss world affairs and contemporary issues. The understanding of these often complex issues is another form of substantive knowledge that language teachers need to gain so they can confidently discuss it with their students.

Languages also have procedural knowledge. This is an understanding of how all the words and phrases fit together to make meaning. Without this knowledge it will be impossible to construct sentences and to communicate effectively. It is the skill of translating, or the skill of reading, listening, writing and speaking in the language. It requires a learner to know which words to use and in what order and how to use key phrases. The utilisation of this knowledge relies on having substantive knowledge to draw on in the first place.

Languages as a powerful knowledge

It could be argued that the Classics education community failed to make the case as to why their subjects are significant for young people and, as a result, ceased to exist in most schools. Yet numbers of students for all languages are falling so there is a need to articulate their educational importance. But powerful knowledge may not be the best way to make the argument. One of the key characteristics of powerful knowledge is that there is a strong link to the parent academic discipline, so any knowledge created can be replaced by 'better' knowledge. The relationship to university language departments is not as simple as in other subjects.

Languages evolve through the people who speak them, not through new discoveries in academic research. This lack of a clear link to a strong research field has led Freeman and Johnson (1998: 404) to explain that language teaching has not 'defined its own forms of knowledge'. As they explain:

. . . .

Language teaching ... has not actively pursued and defined its own forms of knowledge. Instead, the field has depended on the familiar forms of research and documentation of its parent disciplines in the social sciences ... These forms have largely failed to penetrate the domain of the classroom and thus remain largely dysfunctional to teachers themselves. (Freeman and Johnson, 1998: 404)

. . . .

Yet there are ways in which the school subject is informed by advances in the academic disciplines. Ashbee (2021) acknowledges that ideas around syntax and language morphology have been studied by academics at a high level. The associated academic fields of linguistics and studies in literature (in languages other than English) provide insights which can be of use to a languages teacher, but the idea that the academic field is somehow providing 'better' knowledge for teachers (as it might for science) does not fit.

The three futures heuristic provides another means to articulate the value and contemporary challenges of languages education. A Future 1 languages curriculum would see languages as inert and never changing. There would be a focus on the learning and recitation of facts, perhaps frequent vocabulary tests and grammar exercises but devoid of any sort of broader context for the language in terms of place or culture. Classical languages, such as Latin, have historically placed a real emphasis on grammar and vocabulary, but if this is done at the expense of, for example, learning about Roman life or ancient Greece or reading original texts, then there is a danger that Future 1 thinking dominates the discourse. Future 1 thinking fits nicely in an output-driven curriculum in which measurable progress can be recorded and tracked. Critics of the knowledge-led curriculum that pervaded much of the 2010s have accused languages education of following this thinking. As Shirley Lawes (2021: 130) explains, 'Learning a foreign language does not fit comfortably in an "outcomes"-driven curriculum where short-term goals and "evidence-gathering" prevails.' For Lawes, Future 1 thinking is too narrow and constrictive. It strips languages of their humanity, reducing them to a set of vocabulary to learn, grammar rules to recite and predictable conversations to enact.

A Future 2 languages curriculum would see an overemphasis on generic competencies at the expense of developing good language knowledge. The art of communication would be a more significant aim than being able to apply the rules of grammar correctly. As long as a student can go into a café in France and order the correct coffee, then this will suffice as a successful outcome of French education. Yet there is a greater danger of curricular corruption here. When speaking a language, students need something to discuss. Whereas in a Future 1 curriculum this would be predictable safe topics that have been selected to practise specific vocabulary – like 'at the seaside' or 'in the shop' – suddenly with Future 2 thinking there are no rules about what can and cannot be discussed. Students would be discussing all manner of issues such as gender awareness, multiculturalism and pollution. These discussions would be taking place in a foreign language and therefore enable development of the language, but under Future 2 thinking the aim is not to learn to speak the language accurately but to take on board specific messages that the teacher wants to promote.

Powerful knowledge is at the heart of a Future 3 curriculum. This rightly needs to contain the substantive and procedural knowledge to enable students to read, speak, listen and write fluently in another language, but it also needs to enable students to learn about the places and the cultures where the language is spoken. Thus, Future 3 thinking takes languages education beyond regular vocabulary testing and grammar practice, key though these are to developing substantive knowledge, towards linking students to other people around the world through shared language. Students can debate a range of contemporary issues in a new language, but the emphasis is on discussion, not on forcing students to take a predetermined position. Reading and sharing songs and poetry written in the target language enables a student to appreciate it more fully than simply reading a translation, through which nuance of meaning or rhythm is often lost. The real potential of languages education, as reflected by Future 3 curriculum thinking, is explained by Lawes (2007: 94):

. . . .

By introducing young people to the culture of a foreign country through the greatest and most creative works that a society or an individual has achieved, we can encourage them to see that there is more to foreign language and culture than the functional and often banal representations they normally experience.

. . . .

It is this Future 3 thinking that can be 'transformative' for a young person (Lawes, 2007) and help develop their capabilities to live in a modern multilingual world.

Teacher voice

MFL

Table 10.1: Results of MFL teacher workshop

School A	School B	School C
Linguistic knowledge – deep understanding of how language works and the ability to apply it to different languages. Understanding cultural differences and our place in the global community. Communicative capabilities – the ability to communicate with people in their native language.	To maintain an open mind towards other cultures (we are the same, yet we are not). Less likely to be fearful if one isn't ignorant. Sharing thoughts and problem solving.	Knowledge and ability to speak a foreign language is a power which opens many doors and makes you a unique learner.

What is striking about these three attempts at expressing the powerful knowledge of modern languages is that they are different but between them cover the various elements of language education as discussed in the literature. Not all teachers seem to prioritise the same ideas. For School C, powerful knowledge comes from the impact that language learning can have on a young person's future. This is expressed in terms of 'opening doors' – a link to a vocational ideology. They also hint at a 'unique' way of learning that makes language education different from other subjects. Whilst this explores areas of pedagogy, rather than simply curriculum, the importance placed on discussion, listening and verbal contributions to lessons is a pedagogy that is unique to language education. School B does not mention knowledge at all, and their third point could apply to a range of subjects, but what they have expressed in the first two parts of their response is the cultural elements of studying language. This is something that Shirley Lawes (2007; 2021) was fearful had been lost in the rush towards a knowledge-led curriculum, yet the idea of becoming open-minded and less ignorant of other people and cultures through language education is expressed as a key aim of their curriculum. School A seems to explore the idea of language knowledge, not for its own sake but to understand other languages, perhaps even helping students to understand more about their own (native) language. Their second point again highlights the cultural aspects of studying languages, with notions of fitting into a global community.

School C offered a vignette which helped to explore their ideas much further:

From the moment the Year 7 (11- and 12-year-old) students enter the classroom they are immersed in the world of Spanish language. The teacher greets them *Hola* and asks them how they are, and they are expected to reply in Spanish, recalling language learnt in a previous lesson. The students are well drilled in opening their exercise books and writing the date and lesson title, also in Spanish. The opening task gets them to link beginnings and endings of words correctly from the board as retrieval practice. The main part of the lesson sees the teacher showing photographs of family groupings (including some same-sex parents and their children). The teacher points to images of grandparents, parents and children, saying and getting the students to repeat new family vocabulary (such as *hermanos*). There is call and response, copying down of key vocabulary and then asking the students if they have any brothers or sisters and what their names are. By the end of the lesson students are confidently asking and answering questions about their own families, and the teacher is circulating the classroom, correcting pronunciation and encouraging responses.

In this small, typical example, students are immersed in a new language. They have gained confidence and learnt more about themselves and their classmates. Language is the most direct connection to other people and cultures. Being able to communicate in another language exposes us to and fosters an appreciation of the traditions, religions, arts and history of the people associated with that language. Greater understanding, in turn, promotes greater tolerance, empathy and acceptance of others – children who have studied another language are more open towards and express more positive attitudes towards the culture associated with that language.

This vignette explores well what can make language education powerful for young people. The 'immersion' of the students in language makes the lesson an experience, and much more than copying down key phrases. The students' routine in terms of writing down the date and lesson title (in Spanish) practises key vocabulary. Much of the lesson requires students to really listen to the teacher. MFL, alongside music, requires students to listen carefully and pick out detail in what they hear, such as correct pronunciation, which can contribute to students' critical listening abilities.

In the lesson outlined, the students were exposed to a range of images of families from around the world – the highlighting of the inclusion of same-sex parents is not done here to instil some sort of moral stance but is simply used as a means to highlight and practise different vocabulary. The central part of the vignette explores the cultural benefits of studying a foreign language in terms of appreciating arts, religions and histories, which, in turn, enables tolerance, empathy and acceptance. This seems very in keeping with many of the discussions in the literature.

Classics

Table 10.2: Results of Classics teacher workshop

School A	School B
Understanding of the languages which form the grammatical and linguistic basis of both English and many other languages.	Deep philosophical and cultural insights.
Reading, in their original text, works of literature which have provided the model for influential works throughout history.	Connection. Cognitive development and focus on logic, decoding, creativity, methodology and accountability.
Opportunity to apprehend the entirety of a culture in its linguistic, historical, philosophical and aesthetic legacy.	Theoretical understanding of origins of thought.
Recognising and evaluating the continuation and development of classical ideals and theories throughout subsequent cultures and civilisations.	

School C is omitted here because it does not have a Classics department. School A and School B suggest cultural understanding as a key facet of the powerful knowledge of Classics education. School A has given examples of what this means – the 'linguistic, historical, philosophical and aesthetic legacy' of past civilisations. Both sets of teachers have linked to philosophies and origins of thought. The ancient Greeks were responsible for some of the biggest ideas in philosophy and maths, and these have been explored elsewhere in this book, Classics enables students to read this work in its original format. School A is keen to express Classics in terms of contemporary studies and links to modern languages. Knowing, for example, that the word *aqua* in Latin means 'water' helps students to understand words like 'aquarium' in English or *agua* in Spanish. Neither school identifies knowledge of vocabulary or grammar as an expression of powerful knowledge, although perhaps that is what School B means by 'decoding'.

Conclusions: towards languages capabilities

An ambitious Future 3 languages curriculum includes a deep understanding of both the substantive and procedural knowledge of how to speak, listen, read and write in a language, as well as an understanding of the culture of the people who speak it. A Future 3 curriculum does not prioritise one over the other. Ruth Ashbee (2021: 87) expresses this well when she says: 'Knowing, and living-in, a foreign language bring us insights into human existence, the logic, structure, and features of language, and concepts of meaning and representation.'

The linguistic elements of vocabulary learning and practice are significant in developing a core of knowledge, but this is not an end in itself, as proponents of Future 1 thinking might maintain. Some have argued that the recent knowledge turn has created an overfocus on the measurable aspects of the curriculum – being able to translate and speak at the expense of using the language to open minds to culture. An overemphasis on using languages to inculcate a set of values would be Future 2 thinking. Language education becomes a means to get students to think in set ways about healthy eating, for example. The balance is where the Future 3 curriculum can be realised. Students can learn vocabulary to engage in range of contemporary issues, but the focus is on being able to communicate effectively and discussing the issues in the language. The teacher voices identified the unique role that languages can play in connecting people to other people and places, but what they were not able to articulate was a meaningful example of how this occurs.

Based on the literature and teachers' input, languages (both modern and classical) can be considered powerful for young people through the following expression:

? Deep analytical knowledge of the structure and morphology of language. This includes the vast and ever-changing substantive and procedural knowledge of vocabulary, the rules of grammar, and the ability to translate passages of text into and from other languages to determine meaning.

? For modern languages, the knowledge required to communicate meaning with other people through a different language. This requires attention not just to the written form of the language but also to aural pronunciation and deep listening.

? An appreciation of the links between language and the places where that language is spoken (or was spoken historically). This includes geography, politics and culture, which can include art, music, cuisine and fashion. For classical languages this is about civilisations long gone – namely ancient Greece and Rome – and for modern languages it is about countries and, for many European powers, their former colonies and international territories which still speak the language.

It is by focusing on these aspects that young people's capabilities can be developed. These include a critical stance on the nuance of translation and language, and cultural understanding and increased tolerance of people around the world.

There are still real challenges in schools over which languages should be included in a contemporary curriculum. A refocus on why languages are there in the first place and what they seek to help a young person achieve might help school leaders to make these important decisions.

For discussion

? What languages are on offer for students in your school? What has informed that decision?

? What languages should be on offer for young people, and why?

? What role might dead languages like ancient Greek and Latin play in a modern curriculum?

? Should schools abandon German in favour of Mandarin?

? Which is more important, getting students to speak, listen to, read and write a language fluently or getting students to appreciate the culture of the places that speak it?

? If you use languages to explore complex issues such as climate change, how important is it that what you are discussing is scientifically accurate?

? Reflect on the expression of the powerful knowledge of languages given in the conclusion to this chapter. Would you adapt or change it? Might this look different for different languages? Could you refine it for French or Latin?

Chapter 11

What might make physical education a powerful knowledge?

Those of us who were living in the UK during summer 2012 will never forget the London Olympic and Paralympic Games. Most of the sporting events were focused around the impressive Olympic Park in East London, which had transformed the area beyond recognition in the seven years since London won the bid to host the Games. The streets of London became the backdrop to the marathon, leafy Surrey for the cycling and the sea off the coast of Weymouth for the sailing. The summer of sport galvanised a nation, showcased much that was great about the country and inspired a nation of young people to get out of the house, off their computers and trying out some sport. As well as the obvious physical and economic development of some of the most deprived areas of the capital, another aim of the games was to promote a love of sport amongst young people. For a nation home to some of the unhealthiest teenagers in Europe (Roberts, 2010), this was a drive to improve public health. PE teachers in schools were, of course, key to the success of delivering on this aim, providing time and opportunity for students to increase their physical activities. There were many Olympic-themed curricular activities produced by a range of organisations for different subjects to inspire schoolchildren.

This ambitious aim, to increase young people's physical activity, was hampered by a series of ill-timed headlines. News outlets were reporting that school leaders were selling off playing fields, reducing the space for students be active (as reported in *The Guardian*: Vasagar and Herbert, 2012). This was due to a toxic combination of a housing crisis which saw increased pressures on space for new developments, a tightening of school funding which meant that selling off land was a means to gain extra revenue, and a loosening of the laws around green belt restrictions which made it easier for house-building companies to have planning applications accepted.

Alongside this was a political climate which saw increased attention given to educational achievement in a narrow range of academic subjects. Time given to English, maths and science was often increased, which saw time for subjects like PE reduced. Just when the emphasis on school sport should have been increasing to capture the cultural zeitgeist, the time and space afforded to it was reduced in real terms.

The 2012 London Olympics did have some success in promoting healthy lifestyles. The success of the British Cycling team, with gold medals for Bradley Wiggins, led to an increase in sales of bicycles (Davies, 2012) and the number of people out on their bikes. Yet the long-term legacy of the Olympic Games in terms of a surge of interest in school PE is more questionable.

Scientists have made tangible links between exercise, diet and fitness and a long and happy life (e.g. Schubert and Broom, 2020). Maintaining a healthy lifestyle has long been known to be beneficial for humans. During childhood and adolescence, physical activity actively helps young people's brains to develop healthily, which improves all cognitive abilities (Hillman et al., 2020). Students who exercise are giving themselves the best chance to succeed academically. Active teenagers are more likely to go on to be fit and healthy adults – reducing the burden on health services – who are able to contribute to the workforce more fervently and live long and fulfilling lives. Given the significance of physical activity, especially during the early years, the role of the PE teacher should be one of the most significant in any school.

Childhood obesity is increasing in what medical experts have described as an imminent pandemic in the developed world (e.g. Lancet, 2022), and whilst this cannot be blamed on a lack of school sports, the role of education in helping young people to understand diet, fitness and health choices provides one important rationale for the inclusion of PE in the curriculum.

Physical education in schools

In the UK, the chief medical officer's guidelines recommend that all children and young people aged 5–18 should be engaged in at least sixty minutes of physical activity a day, of which thirty minutes should be at school (Department of Health and Social Care et al., 2019), so there is a statutory requirement for schools to have an active PE programme. Many schools have a games offering alongside more formal PE, but the time given for students to particate in sports varies considerably. Some schools offer all their students two full afternoons of sport a week, as well as an additional PE lesson. Other schools offer far less.

A useful distinction to make is between sport and PE; sport focuses on physical training, skill development and competition whereas PE has a broader, more holistic focus on fitness and wellbeing. The balance between PE and sport, and the extent to which PE should be informed by sport, is a contention at the heart of the school subject.

Rush Ashbee (2021: 101) describes PE as being 'unique amongst the school subjects in that one of its main, explicit goals is participation in addition to the knowledge in the curriculum'. For her, knowledge is just as important a curricular goal as students proactively taking part in sport. This has 'immediate benefits of students' health and well-being, and for the building of lifelong habits in sports and exercise' (Ashbee, 2021: 101). This dual focus on participation and knowledge creates, therefore, an inherent tension in the aim of school PE lessons. Practice vs theory is one of the dualisms that Richard Tinning (2015) identifies in his work on the purpose of school PE. He pinpoints further curricular tensions: whether the aim of PE is to encourage wide participation for general health, to teach students about the various socio-scientific benefits of physical activity, to coach for elitism in specific sports or to deliver a body of academic knowledge to students.

As Tinning (2015: 680) argues:

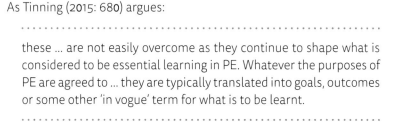

these ... are not easily overcome as they continue to shape what is considered to be essential learning in PE. Whatever the purposes of PE are agreed to ... they are typically translated into goals, outcomes or some other 'in vogue' term for what is to be learnt.

Tinning suggests that the holistic aims of PE are translated too readily into measurable outcomes when applied to schools. In response, he offers 'Bildung vs vocational' (Tinning, 2015: 680) as another dualism, which looks at the tensions between the more holistic health benefits of PE against more measurable outcomes with tangible links to specific jobs. The European tradition of Bildung has strong links to the idea of capabilities as discussed in this book.

The nature of school PE has changed over time with an increasingly academic focus in recent decades. The introduction of GCSE and A level courses means students are tested under exam conditions on a range of knowledge requirements. PE teachers need to be more than simply good sports performers; they are expected to have a well-rounded understanding of elements of sports science, such as anatomy and physiology, as well as the rules of various sports and activities. On top of this, PE teachers need to understand the wider benefits that their subject can bring to young people.

Yet even if students are simply participating in sports, they will still be developing knowledge: knowledge of the game they are playing, its rules and procedures; knowledge of the various game play tactics needed to improve performance; knowledge of teamwork and cooperation. There is also the notion of self-knowledge, a realisation of the benefits of fitness, which can lead to desire for further growth and physical development.

PE as a procedural knowledge

Given the focus on participation and being active, PE is often thought of as a practical skills subject, with the skill being the ability to perform in a particular sport. The basis of this skill is the procedural knowledge, the know-how, an understanding of how to do the sport. Thus, the procedural knowledge of PE is potentially vast as it encompasses all the sports taught.

Knowing how to play a particular sport is one thing, but practising skills to a level where they become embedded is another, and it is this which can be considered a form of embodied knowledge (e.g. Francesconi and Gallagher, 2019). A player becomes so physically and emotionally absorbed in a game that they are using their skills almost without actively thinking. It is a dynamic and enacted knowledge that can only really be reached through continual practice and development. This way of thinking about knowledge in sport has developed from the fields of cognitive science and sport psychology, as it also includes ideas such as confidence and self-belief.

One challenge for teachers regards how much procedural knowledge, and the skills practice that follows, needs to be taught for each sport, especially if the aim is to develop embodied knowledge. The same physical activity could be repeated over and over, the students would become skilled in that activity and may well be able to achieve high status in the sport, but this would be at the expense of trying other activities. On the other hand, if students are trying out a new sport or activity each week, they may never be able to achieve success in one. This push towards encouraging 'elite' performance rather than developing broader basic competence was researched by Solvason (2010: 122), who argued:

. . . .

there has been a subtle but significant shift in emphasis away from inclusion and towards elitism in sports ... Equality of educational provision became overshadowed by a rather more selective drive towards excellence.

. . . .

The balance between providing procedural knowledge that will enable all students to feel included in physical activity, and at the same time ensuring that those with ability and interest in the sport are able to be recognised and given opportunities to practise and develop, is a curricular decision that teachers need to make.

PE as a substantive knowledge

Richard Tinning's (2015) observation that PE can't agree on its subject matter is in part due to the lack of overall aims for the subject in schools. Despite this, Ruth Ashbee (2021) identifies types of substantive knowledge in school PE: knowledge of theory – such as physiology, nutrition, sports psychology and anatomy; knowledge of the structures of sport and physical activities – the rules and traditions of various sports; alongside the procedural knowledge needed to develop physical skill and abilities – such as speed, agility, ball handling, and so forth.

Substantive knowledge is that identifiable set of core knowledge – the knowledge of the various theories that underlie the subject. The main challenge for school PE is that that the subject itself is a curricular construction rather than an actively researched university discipline. The subject of kinesiology – the study of human movement – has provided a knowledge basis for PE, but over time the subject has drawn from more formal sports science programmes. Part of this shift has been to increase the acceptance of the subject as worthy of study in an educational landscape that increasingly values academics above all else. The lack of academic value in PE has long been identified. Writing about undergraduate programmes for sport, Daryl Siedentop (2002: 372) says:

the direct study of sport skill and strategy ... is not considered to be of sufficient academic quality to form the core of an undergraduate degree program ... If we cannot confront that core problem, and somehow resolve it, then physical education in schools is doomed.

By way of a solution to this challenge, he identifies some ways in which school PE develops knowledge:

The teacher of physical education and the coach of children and youth sport teams need to have a reasonable mastery of the sport activities they will teach to their students and players – that is their content knowledge. They should know the technical aspects of the skills involved ... And, they should 'know' these things intellectually and as performers, each kind of knowledge having its own meaning. (Siedentop, 2002: 374)

The substantive knowledge of PE, therefore, derives from the rules of the various sporting activities that students take part in. Whilst Siedentop is writing about the knowledge that a teacher needs to have, these ideas could equally be seen as valuable to the young people themselves as they learn PE. Students can learn the significance of the sport they are playing to the wider local and national setting. What he does not identify is which activities might be valued as part of this substantive knowledge base. As Tinning (2015: 373) observes:

it has become increasingly clear that 'anything goes' in the name of physical education in schools – units in darts and frisbee having that same substantive value as volleyball and track, with the added appeal of novelty.

. . . .

Deciding which sports to teach to develop students' substantive knowledge of PE is key. In part it will depend on the facilities available. Those schools fortunate enough to have the use of a swimming pool will be able to offer a swimming programme; those who are close to an athletics track will benefit from this. Teachers have important decisions to make about how to deliver the practical programme to students and what it will comprise.

The content of school PE is increasingly drawing from sports science. As a discipline it uses scientific methodologies to increase understanding of sports performance, physicality, psychology and fitness. It draws on other sciences, such as biology, but framed in sports language with evocative words like 'performance' and 'training' being used. This framing is being replicated in school PE textbooks (e.g. Svendsen and Svendsen, 2016).

Students will study biology as a core part of their science curriculum and will learn about the human body, but those who choose to study PE will see how that knowledge can be applied to sports performance. Through collecting and interpreting data – for example, by drawing graphs – a range of mathematical knowledge is practised and developed too.

Despite this increased academicisation of school PE, a number of writers have criticised the sports-led approach as reinforcing a range of social inequalities (as summarised and discussed in Svendsen and Svendsen, 2016). These include a reinforcement of gender inequalities. Some sports are perceived to be for girls, such as netball, and others perceived to be for boys, such as rugby. The writers make a similar argument for social class – for example, football, rugby and cricket might attract different supporters based on socio-economic background. The perception of who is able to take part in which sport is reinforced by the media through advertising and sponsorship, which can affect the decisions taken by teachers in schools. Despite their huge successes in the national game, women's football still trails well behind the men's game in terms of revenue in the UK, and this affects the nature of who plays football in schools. Since the success of the England women's team in the European Championships in 2022 and World Cup in 2023, more girls are now wanting to play football but provision in schools varies (Women in Sport, 2024).

PE as a powerful knowledge

PE has the potential to reap real benefits for young people in their understanding of themselves and the world. Yet expressing the ways in which it might be powerful knowledge is more problematic. Armour and Jones (1998: 85) have argued that PE as a subject 'may be trying to do too much', and it is this tension that leads to a tendency not to change.

Firstly, there are no PE researchers in universities, and this provides a challenge for the concept of powerful knowledge. Capel and Blair (2007: 3) have explained why this might be problematic for teachers:

> Because the theoretical nature of sport sciences degrees does not prepare students for the practical nature of physical education as taught in schools, trainee teachers rely on knowledge gained from experience outside their degree course for teaching the curriculum.

Their observation is that trainee teachers tend towards the continuation of the status quo, by following what their placement school has always done, rather than thinking more broadly about how PE can be transformational for young people. They continue:

> If physical education is going to meet the needs of young people today, it is argued that we need physical education teachers ... who can challenge and, where appropriate, change the teaching of the subject. (Capel and Blair, 2007: 7)

A curriculum which is focused on developing powerful knowledge could help overcome some of the many challenges identified regarding traditional models of teaching excluding certain groups and making assumptions about who can take part in which sports.

Teacher voice

Table 11.1: Results of PE teacher workshop

School A	School B	School C
Skills: problem solving, social skills, communication, teamwork, perseverance. Character: creativity, sportsmanship, fair play, sensitivity. Fitness: understanding of physical literacy. Sport: competition, risk, lifelong passion for an activity.	Builds life skills which are relevant to the world of industry and not necessarily evident in other courses: Presentation skills, debating, marketing, business in sport, careers in sport with the focus on job applications, research methods, current socio-cultural hot topics. Enhance physical performance through training.	Deep understanding of choices that can help lead to an active healthy lifestyle. Theoretically knowing the basics of the human body and how physical activity affects us. Benefits of physical activity – mental, social and physical.

The teachers vary in the ways in which they express the powerful knowledge of PE. School A's approach starts with skills and character, yet neither of these are unique to PE. Many subjects help young people to develop problem-solving skills, social skills, communication, perseverance, creativity and sensitivity. The way in which PE teachers encourage teamwork is different to the sorts of academic group work that might occur in other subjects. Group work in classrooms can develop teamwork, but on a sports field in a competitive game young people are collaborating much more readily and in much faster timeframes, so the development of sports teamwork is a legitimate claim of unique knowledge. This has links to notions of sportsmanship and fair play, which help young people to emotionally regulate wins and losses and follow the rules and spirit of competition. These are some of the personal benefits that could derive from inclusive PE practices.

Physical literacy is a term that School A has identified as a feature of the powerful knowledge; young people develop the substantive knowledge of how to stay fit and active alongside the procedural knowledge of how to get and retain fitness.

School C's approach yields similar results. All three expressions of powerful knowledge describe the holistic benefits of studying the subject. The first expresses the significance of knowledge which gives students the agency to make choices about healthy lifestyles. The second point is similar, but this is the substantive knowledge of human biology, framed in sporting language earlier (Svendsen and Svendsen, 2016). The final part expresses the benefits of physical activity for individuals in terms of their social and mental development.

What neither of the sets of teachers here express is a worry that was identified in some of the literature in terms of 'elitism' and the focus on developing highly skilled sportspeople. It could be implicit in the way their curriculum is constructed, but all the teachers in this study express the curricular value of PE in terms of inclusive physical activities, although none of the teachers here went as far as discussing inclusivity in terms of physical disabilities.

Here is a vignette developed by teachers at School C:

. . . .

Year 9 netball sports session. Students are learning how to pass the ball correctly. They have been taught how to stand, use their feet and the most effective way to pass. As they practise the skill, they will understand the impacts of different movements on their body. They will have learnt about the nature of and importance of fitness through studies of the human body. The physical movement increases their overall fitness and releases endorphins which will have benefits for their mental alertness.

. . . .

This vignette illustrates the real benefits of studying PE. An activity which seems basic, passing a ball, is deconstructed by these teachers into something much more fundamental and powerful for the young people. The students are using the procedural knowledge of how to pass effectively to develop a specific skill which can then be used as part of a game of netball. Ideally, this skill becomes so natural to the student that it becomes embodied knowledge. Yet the real benefit comes through the wider links between this and the substantive knowledge of fitness and the increase in brain activity derived through physical activity, although the extent to which those links are (or need to be) made clear to the students is not discussed here. This vignette illustrates one way in which PE can be considered powerful for young people.

Based on the literature and teacher input, the powerful knowledge of PE could be expressed as:

? Knowledge of the rules of various sports. This includes the laws of the games as well as the physical techniques needed to play them effectively. Embodied knowledge expresses the way in which the procedural knowledge of a particular sport becomes naturalised in players.

? Knowledge of physical literacy and how participation in sport can lead to a healthy lifestyle. This includes the choices a student can make over diet and exercise, the links between these and the impacts on health.

? Knowledge of the self through the development of sportsmanship and teamwork. This includes quick thinking, rapid decision making and reacting to evolving situations.

Conclusions: towards PE capabilities

PE is a core part of young people's experience of school. It contributes to a range of holistic educational capabilities – such as teamwork, leadership, resilience, social development and participation – and these should not be ignored in discussions about the value of PE within the curriculum. An even broader consideration is the contribution that the choice of sports on offer can make to breaking down gender and social imbalances. The inclusive nature of sport offers a collaborative space that is unique in the curriculum, and this is why participation, alongside knowledge, has been identified by Ruth Ashbee (2021) as central to school PE knowledge. Yet these two ideas are not separate, as the teachers expressed in this research. Students need to understand the links between their participation and health, and knowledge plays a key role here.

However, the theory of powerful knowledge aspires to identify the unique educational value of PE. The knowledge basis of PE is significant in helping young people to understand the links between physical activity and their overall health and wellbeing. This knowledge therefore is also knowledge of the self: an understanding of one's own fitness, how to improve it and why. The self-knowledge that arises from PE is linked to notions of emotional control, sportsmanship and fair play, as some of the teachers suggested. The rules of the various sporting activities that students take part in are all part of the wider substantive knowledge of PE that helps to develop personal fitness as well as a range of holistic educational goals. To place it within the ideas of powerful knowledge, the substantive knowledge of fitness, and the framing of human biology in terms of its impacts on fitness, is central to enabling young people to make choices about how to live a healthy life. This seems a key capability to emerge from school PE.

There are many important decisions to be made when developing a school PE curriculum. These have been outlined in this chapter in terms of choices of sports, time and depth devoted to them, the balance of expertise and developing elitism over inclusivity. A focus on the unique value of PE within the curriculum, expressed as powerful knowledge, can help guide PE teachers in making the curriculum valuable and transformational for their students.

For discussion

? What is the difference between PE and sport? What is taught in your school, and how much time/emphasis should be given?

? Is the aim of school sport to develop elite sportspeople or provide inclusive sport for all? Can one school manage both priorities (and, if so, how)?

? How might the idea of embodied knowledge be of use?

? How important is it for PE teachers to be highly skilled in the sport they are teaching?

? Which sports should be included in a PE curriculum and why? How much time should a student spend on a particular sport?

Conclusions: towards a whole-school capabilities curriculum

The ambitious view of education that has been set out in this book is less about making alterations to the way in which schools operate and more about changing the way in which we think about what we are teaching and why. It is easy to dismiss a subject-based curriculum when all it seems to be good for is passing exams and getting students to jump through predetermined societal hoops. It is no wonder that many voices want to ditch subjects altogether and offer students something more inspiring. Yet subject knowledge should be inspiring. This book has argued for the importance of subjects. Not in a tokenistic way that gets in the way of what schools really want to do and to value, but as the central way in which young people are educated. Subjects are empowering.

The expressions of powerful knowledge in Part II can now be used as the basis for curriculum thinking and planning. When a scheme of work is derived for a particular topic, it can be cross-referenced with those ideas. We can check to see that we are teaching what we say we should be.

Back to empowering knowledge of subjects?

This book has used the framework of powerful knowledge to explore notions of knowledge in the classroom. Yet the work with the various subject communities shows that the concept is not so easily transferable across different subjects. There are two elements of powerful knowledge, as Young (2008) expresses it, that are particularly problematic. The first is the idea that there is a tangible link between epistemic communities of experts working in universities and teachers working in schools. Whilst this relationship exists well in the sciences, it is less established in the creative arts and languages, where the real world of artistic creation and expression and the places where language is spoken respectively become the sites for new knowledge.

The second challenge of powerful knowledge comes from the notion of 'better' knowledge. In science this is straightforward, as new theories replace older ones. But it is a messy process in the arts and literature. Rather than there being better knowledge on offer, there is often different knowledge, and a range of equally valid ways of interpreting and knowing. There is often talk of knowledges in the plural. Recent work on decolonising the curriculum has shown this to be particularly important.

These criticisms of powerful knowledge were explored in earlier chapters but have been shown in the ways in which teachers have struggled to engage with the concept. Perhaps John White's (2019) ideas around a language of specialised knowledges, rather than powerful knowledge, might be more appropriate in some subjects. Yet powerful knowledge is a pervasive construct, and it is the ways in which it can provide power for young people that make it such an enticing idea. It is the ways in which subjects can be empowering in some way for young people that is the central claim of this book. Students learn knowledge, skills and values through engagement with their subjects and this develops a range of educational capabilities; it is these that can be empowering for young people.

What might educational capabilities look like?

In his work on the capability approach, Sen (2004) never endorsed a list of capabilities as he argued that this should be done in specific contexts. The same could be said for educational capabilities. It is up to school leaders to decide on the sorts of qualities and abilities that they want the young people in their charge to emerge with. Often, these are wrapped up in the form of slick slogans or mission statements. Finding tangible links between these soundbites and the real work of the curriculum can be challenging. If the sort of curriculum thinking that this book encourages really does exist in schools, then a range of educational capabilities seems to emerge naturally. From the various teacher voices and the experts from the literature, a range of possible educational capabilities emerges.

A Future 3 curriculum based on the powerful knowledge of subjects (as problematic as that term might be for some) can lead to the following tentative list of educational capabilities:

？ **Capabilities associated with students finding new ways to make sense of themselves and the world.** Through the knowledge and skills that students gain they are able to know themselves and know the world. Educated young people will know things, and will have engaged with some of the greatest ideas that humanity has ever produced. This includes great works of art and technology, the greatest scientific discoveries and the greatest sporting achievements. They will have the language with which to discuss and make sense of this knowledge and an understanding that this knowledge is only ever tentative as new ways of making meaning emerge. In turn, this contributes to students' cultural capital – their ability to engage meaningfully in the great debates of our time.

？ **Capabilities associated with different claims to truth.** Educated young people will be able to challenge the sources of data and information presented to them. They can identify fact from fiction. This is particularly pertinent in an era of fake news, online filter bubbles and indiscriminate AI.

？ **Capabilities associated with critical thinking.** Young people will know how claims to truth in science are different to claims to truth in the arts. Critical thinking can include understanding how knowledge is made in different subjects. Critical thinking is a different process in science than in literature but it can seek to challenge the nature of truth and claims about the world.

？ **Capabilities associated with choices about how to live and work.** Young people can actively make decisions about the sorts of work they are able and want to do, what they want to study and how they want to spend their leisure time. They can make choices about exercise, diet and fitness. They are individual and autonomous and free to think and reason. This comes from a position of strength and personal responsibility, knowing themselves and being at ease with the choices they are able to make.

？ **Capabilities associated with agency.** Students will encounter issues and develop values in their education, and knowledge of this can inspire a response. A young person can be radical and can take action to envision the sort of future they want to create for themselves. This is not something drilled into them uncritically but something nurtured. It might mean taking an ethical stance on a political issue or having the knowledge to engage with local decision making. It might mean making choices about personal consumption of goods, food, fuel, and more or taking responsibility for planetary stewardship. It is about being an active and engaged citizen of the world.

How do we get there?

Enabling a Future 3 curriculum in practice requires a change in thinking. Whilst many of the teachers who provide their voices in Part II talk eloquently about their subjects, it is easy for this sentiment to get lost in a curriculum which seeks to reduce schools to exam factories.

If we are serious about enabling a Future 3, powerful-knowledge-led capabilities curriculum to flourish, then the following conditions are needed (the various conditions here are based on Bustin, 2019: 184–187):

? **A subject-based curriculum.** The empowering knowledge of subjects should drive the school curriculum. Everything else that school leaders are wanting to achieve should stem from this. This means not combining subjects to reduce teaching time. It means resisting selling off assets like sports pitches. It means ensuring that students have access to a rigorous curriculum with a range of diverse subjects. It means students should be studying the full range of subjects to the end of Year 9 and not dropping some to start GCSEs a year early.

? **Subject specialists in front of every class.** If we are serious about not just teaching the information required to pass exams but inducting students into subjects' ways of thinking, then specialist teachers are required. These specialists need to know their subjects, have completed degree-level study, and continue to access subject specialist professional development throughout their careers to remain at the forefront of their subject and the pedagogies needed to teach it effectively.

? **A focus on outcomes not outputs.** The measurable outputs of the curriculum in the form of examination grades have come to dominate, at the expense of developing the broader knowledge, skills and values on which capabilities can develop. These outcomes can be gained from a deep immersion in school subjects, and it is this that can enable greater educational capabilities. It is not that examinations are unimportant; they provide a useful role in education, but they should not be the beating heart of a school.

？ **Focus on curriculum as well as pedagogy.** In Mark and Zoe Enser's (2021) book, *The CPD Curriculum: Creating Conditions for Growth,* they argue that career professional development is not something that is done to tick a box but should be engrained in the professional work of teachers. So much time is given over to explorations of how to teach that often the deeper questions about what we are teaching and why can be lost or not considered. Developing a Future 3 curriculum requires deep thought, but teachers need to return to it often and to refine their thinking. School leaders need to afford the time and support to enable this.

？ **Curriculum coherence.** The language of capabilities can be used to unite what could otherwise be a very disparate experience for students in school. Each subject is unique and has its own claims to truth and value in schooling, but capabilities can provide some form of unity. This is not about making crude links between subjects where there are none, but acknowledging and celebrating that differences exist between subjects and how they each contribute to making a young person a capable, free, autonomous individual. This should, of course, be reflected in the various mission statements and promotional materials that schools use to market themselves.

？ **Teachers as professional curriculum makers.** If we are to value the work of specialist teachers, then we need to give them the space to innovate and create. Teachers are the curriculum makers; teachers know their subjects and know their students. As such, we need to trust teachers to create their own curriculum – to create their own lesson plans. This means not providing a package of material for them to deliver uncritically but trusting them as professionals. Teaching is a profession requiring post-graduate study, and if we are serious about creating the space for Future 3 thinking then it needs to remain that way.

Final conclusions

This book has argued that every young person is entitled to a powerful-knowledge-led, subject-based curriculum. This entitlement is why the debates are wrapped up in ideas around social justice. The list of educational capabilities presented here has been drawn from the literature and teacher voices but is designed to be partial and tentative. It is intended to start conversations in schools about what is valued and how subjects are able to drive that thinking.

The ambition of curriculum thinking presented in this book might seem beyond the reach of individual teachers. After all, we cannot change the examination system, nor the high stakes that are placed on it by students, parents and wider society. Nor can we change the challenges of recruitment and the other broader challenges that the profession faces. Sometimes we have to teach subjects that are outside of our expertise. Sometimes we have to focus on exam technique to help students understand the difference between assessment objective 1 and assessment objective 2. Sometimes we have to focus on routines and behaviour so we are able to teach something!

Yet if we allow this to become the norm and the end point of our thinking, then we lose sight of what we are trying to do. This book has argued that as teachers we are the curriculum makers. We are able to see the bigger educational picture; we can link what we are teaching Year 9 on a Monday morning with a broader set of educational capabilities that they will possess as they walk out into the world. This should be an empowering thought, not just for them but for us too.

For discussion

? How might the expressions of powerful knowledge of individual subjects contribute in some way to broader whole-school capabilities?

? How do you respond to the list of capabilities presented here? What is missing? What is not needed?

? If you are a school leader with responsibility for whole-school marketing, how might the ideas presented here provide a whole-school vision of curriculum?

? If you are a school leader, how can you inspire and support your teachers to develop the sort of curriculum thinking outlined here?

References

Alkire, S. (2002). *Valuing Freedoms: Sen's Capability Approach and Poverty Reduction*. Oxford: Oxford University Press.

Anderson, E. (2016). *The Invention of Science: A New History of the Scientific Revolution* by David Wootton [review]. *Ethnobiology Letters*, 7(1): 55–58.

Armour, K. and Jones, R. (1998). *Physical Education Teachers' Lives and Careers: PE, Sport and Educational Status*. London: Falmer Press.

Ashbee, R. (2021). *Curriculum: Theory, Culture and the Subject Specialisms*. Abingdon: Routledge.

Baker, D. (2014). *The Schooled Society: The Educational Transformation of Global Culture*. Redwood City, CA: Stanford University Press.

Bates, G. (2021). Chemistry. In A. Sehgal Cuthbert and A. Standish (eds), *What Should Schools Teach? Disciplines, Subjects and the Pursuit of Truth*, 2nd edn. London: UCL Press, pp. 202–217.

BBC News (1999). Bard is millennium man (1 January). Available at: http://news.bbc.co.uk/1/hi/uk/245752.stm.

BBC News (2013). Obama: no time for a meeting of the Flat Earth Society (25 June). Available at: https://www.bbc.co.uk/news/av/world-us-canada-23057369.

BBC News (2017). Banksy's balloon girl chosen as nation's favourite artwork (26 July). Available at: https://www.bbc.co.uk/news/uk-england-40717821.

BBC News (2020). Shakespeare First Folio fetches a record $10 million at auction (14 October). Available at: https://www.bbc.co.uk/news/entertainment-arts-54544737.

BBC News (2021). Banksy's Love is in the Bin sells for a record £16 million (14 October). Available at: https://www.bbc.com/news/entertainment-arts-58908768.amp?s=08.

BCS (2022). Record numbers of students choose computer science A level in 2022 (22 June). Available at: https://www.bcs.org/articles-opinion-and-research/record-numbers-of-students-choose-computer-science-a-level-in-2022.

Berglund, F. and Reiss, M. J. (2021). Biology. In A. Sehgal Cuthbert and A. Standish (eds), *What Should Schools Teach? Disciplines, Subjects and the Pursuit of Truth*, 2nd edn. London: UCL Press, pp. 189–201.

Bernstein, B. (2000). *Pedagogy, Symbolic Control and Identity: Theory, Research and Critique*, rev. edn. London: Taylor and Francis.

Biesta, G. (2013). Giving teaching back to education: responding to the disappearance of the teacher. *Phenomenology and Practice*, 6(2): 35–49.

Boaler, J. (2010). *The Elephant in the Classroom: Helping Children Learn and Love Maths*. London: Souvenir Press.

Bonnett, A. (2008). *What is Geography?* London: Sage.

British Educational Research Association (2018). *Ethical Guidelines for Educational Research*, 4th edn. London: BERA. Available at: https://www.bera.ac.uk/publication/ethical-guidelines-for-educational-research-2018.

Bryant, M. (2021). Latin to be introduced at 40 state secondaries in England. *The Guardian* (31 July). Available at: https://www.theguardian.com/education/2021/jul/31/latin-introduced-40-state-secondaries-england.

Bube, A. (2021). Educational potentials of embodied art reflection. *Phenomenology and the Cognitive Sciences*, 20(4): 423–441.

Bustin, R. (2017a). An investigation into Geocapability and Future 3 curriculum thinking in geography. PhD thesis, UCL Institute of Education. Available at: https://discovery.ucl.ac.uk/id/eprint/1549680/1/Bustin_R_thesis.pdf.

Bustin, R. (2017b). Teaching a good geography lesson. In M. Jones (ed.), *The Handbook of Secondary Geography*. Sheffield: Geographical Association, pp. 134–149.

Bustin, R. (2019). *Geography Education's Potential and the Capability Approach: GeoCapabilities and Schools*. London: Palgrave Macmillan.

Butler, N. M. (1948). Introduction. In M. Newmark (ed.), *Twentieth Century Modern Language Teaching: Sources and Readings*. New York: The Philosophical Library.

Bustin, R., Butler, K. and Hawley, D. (2017). GeoCapabilities: teachers as curriculum leaders. *Teaching Geography*, 42(1): 18–22.

Capel, S. and Blair, R. (2007). Moving beyond physical education subject knowledge to develop knowledgeable teachers of the subject. *Curriculum Journal*, 18(4): 493–507.

Chapman, A. (ed.) (2021a). *Knowing History in Schools: Powerful Knowledge and the Powers of Knowledge*. London: UCL Press.

Chapman, A. (2021b). Introduction: historical knowing and the 'knowledge turn'. In A. Chapman (ed.), *Knowing History in Schools: Powerful Knowledge and the Powers of Knowledge*. London: UCL Press, pp. 1–31.

Civitas (2007). Corruption of the curriculum [press release] (11 June). Available at: https://www.civitas.org.uk/press/corruption-of-the-curriculum.

Claxton, G. (2018). *The Learning Power Approach: Teaching Learners to Teach Themselves*. Carmarthen: Crown House Publishing.

Collen, I. (2023). *Language Trends 2023: Language Teaching in Primary and Secondary Schools in England*. London: British Council. Available at: https://www.britishcouncil.org/sites/default/files/language_trends_england_2023.pdf.

Counsell, C. (2021). History. In A. Sehgal Cuthbert and A. Standish (eds), *What Should Schools Teach? Disciplines, Subjects and the Pursuit of Truth*, 2nd edn. London: UCL Press, pp. 154–173.

Crisan, C. (2021). Mathematics. In A. Sehgal Cuthbert and A. Standish (eds), *What Should Schools Teach? Disciplines, Subjects and the Pursuit of Truth*, 2nd edn. London: UCL Press, pp. 234–250.

Davies, L. (2012). Bradley Wiggins London 2012 triumph brings boost to British cycling. *The Guardian* (2 August). Available at: https://www.theguardian.com/sport/2012/aug/02/bradley-wiggins-london-2012-triumph-boosts-cycling.

Davis, W. (2009). *The Wayfinders: Why Ancient Wisdom Matters in the Modern World (CBC Massey Lecture)*. Toronto, ON: House of Anansi Press.

Department for Education (2014). Promoting fundamental British values through SMSC: departmental advice for maintained schools. DFE-00679-2014 (November). Available at: https://www.gov.uk/government/publications/promoting-fundamental-british-values-through-smsc.

Department for Education (2021). National curriculum in England: mathematics programmes of study. Available at: https://www.gov.uk/government/publications/national-curriculum-in-england-mathematics-programmes-of-study/national-curriculum-in-england-mathematics-programmes-of-study.

Department for Education and Gibb, N. (2018). School standards minister at ResearchED [speech] (8 September). Available at: https://www.gov.uk/government/speeches/school-standards-minister-at-researched.

Department for Education and Gibb, N. (2021). The importance of a knowledge rich curriculum [speech] (21 July). Available at: https://www.gov.uk/government/speeches/the-importance-of-a-knowledge-rich-curriculum.

Department of Health and Social Care, Llwodraeth Cymru Welsh Government, Department of Health Northern Ireland and the Scottish Government (2019). *UK Chief Medical Officers' Physical Activity Guidelines* (7 September). Available at: https://assets.publishing.service.gov.uk/government/uploads/system/uploads/attachment_data/file/832868/uk-chief-medical-officers-physical-activity-guidelines.pdf.

Dewey, J. (1934). *Art as Experience*. New York: Minton, Balch and Company.

Dorling, D. and Lee, C. (2016). *Geography: Ideas in Profile*. London: Profile Books.

Dowling, P. (1998). *The Sociology of Mathematics Education: Mathematical Myths/Pedagogic Texts*. London: Falmer Press.

Duell, M. and Wright, J. (2021). Grammar school head issues 'unequivocal apology' and suspends 'RE teacher who showed class Prophet Muhammad cartoon' – but sends police officer out to tell furious Muslim parents protesting at front gates. *Mail Online* (31 March). Available at: https://www.dailymail.co.uk/news/article-9401527/Furious-parents-protest-Prophet-Muhammad-cartoon-shown-class.html.

Dweck, C. (2017). *Growth Mindset: Changing the Way You Think to Fulfil Your Potential.* London: Robinson.

Dyvik, E. H. (2024). The most spoken languages worldwide in 2023. *Statista* (21 June). Available at: https://www.statista.com/statistics/266808/the-most-spoken-languages-worldwide.

Eaglestone, R. (2021). 'Powerful knowledge', 'cultural literacy' and the study of literature in schools. *Impact*, 26: 2–41. Available at: https://onlinelibrary.wiley.com/doi/epdf/10.1111/2048-416X.2020.12006.x.

Education Scotland (2017). What is Curriculum for Excellence? (1 January). Available at: https://education.gov.scot/curriculum-for-excellence/about-curriculum-for-excellence/what-is-curriculum-for-excellence.

Education Wales (2020). Developing a vision for curriculum design (28 January). Available at: https://hwb.gov.wales/curriculum-for-wales/designing-your-curriculum/developing-a-vision-for-curriculum-design.

Eisner, E. (2008). Art and knowledge. In J. G. Knowles and A. L. Cole (eds), *Handbook of the Arts in Qualitative Research: Perspectives, Methodologies, Examples, and Issues.* London: Sage, pp. 3–12.

Elkins, J. (2001). *Why Art Cannot Be Taught: A Handbook for Art Students.* Champaign, IL: University of Illinois Press.

Elkins, J. (ed.) (2012). *What Do Artists Know? Volume 3: Stone Art Theory Institutes.* University Park, PA: Pennsylvania State University Press.

Enser, M. (2021). *Powerful Geography: A Curriculum with Purpose in Practice.* Carmarthen: Crown House Publishing.

Enser, M. and Enser, Z. (2021). *The CPD Curriculum: Creating Conditions for Growth.* Carmarthen: Crown House Publishing.

Erduran, S. (2001). Philosophy of chemistry: an emerging field with implications for chemistry education. *Science and Education*, 10(6): 581–593.

Erikson, R. (1998). Award ceremony speech, 10 December. Available at: https://www.nobelprize.org/prizes/economic-sciences/1998/ceremony-speech.

Fisher, P. (2000). *Thinking Through History.* Cambridge: Chris Kington Publishing.

Forrest, M. (1996). *Modernising the Classics.* Exeter: University of Exeter Press.

Freeman, D. and Johnson, K. (1998). Reconceptualizing the knowledge-base of language teacher education. *TESOL Quarterly*, 32(3): 397–417.

Furedi, F. (2007). Introduction: politics, politics, politics. In R. Whelan (ed.), *The Corruption of the Curriculum.* London: Civitas, pp. 1–10.

Gericke, N., Hudson, B., Olin-Scheller, C. and Stolare, M. (2018). Powerful knowledge, transformations and the need for empirical studies across school subjects. *London Review of Education*, 16: 428–444.

Gibney, D. (2018). Towards an ideal chemistry curriculum: framing the secondary science curriculum. *SSR*, 100(370): 30–35. Available at: https://www.ase.org.uk/system/files/SSR_September_2018_30-35_Gibney.pdf.

Global Bildung Network (2021). Better Bildung, Better Future: A Bildung Manifesto for a Global Renaissance 2.0 (9 May). Available at: https://www.globalbildung.net/manifesto.

Goodson, I. (2005). *Learning, Curriculum and Life History: The Selected Works of Ivor F. Goodson.* Abingdon: Routledge.

Goudie, A. (1993). Schools and universities – the great divide. *Geography*, 78(4): 338–339.

Hafez, R. (2021). Religious education. In A. Sehgal Cuthbert and A. Standish (eds), *What Should Schools Teach? Disciplines, Subjects and the Pursuit of Truth*, 2nd edn. London: UCL Press, pp. 174–188.

Hand, M. (2021). Editorial introduction. In R. Eaglestone, 'Powerful knowledge', 'cultural literacy' and the study of literature in schools. *Impact*, 26: 2–4. Available at: https://onlinelibrary.wiley.com/doi/epdf/10.1111/2048-416X.2020.12006.x.

Hayes, D. P. (1992). The growing inaccessibility of science. *Nature*, 356: 739–740.

Hillman, C. H., McDonald, K. M. and Logan, N. E. (2020). A review of the effects of physical activity on cognition and brain health across children and adolescence. *Nestle Nutrition Institute Workshop Series*, 95: 116–126.

Hinchliffe, G. (2006). Beyond key skills: exploring capabilities. Presentation given on 16 June to Networking Day for Humanities Careers Advisers in London. Available at: https://slideplayer.com/slide/7916968.

Hirsch, E. D. (1967). *Validity in Interpretation*. New Haven, CT: Yale University Press.

Hirsch, E. D. (1988). *Cultural Literacy: What Every American Needs to Know*. New York: Random House.

Hirsch, E. D. (2014). *What Your Year 6 Child Needs to Know: Fundamentals of a Good Year 6 Education*. London: Civitas.

Hordern, J. (2019). Exercise and intervention: on the sociology of powerful knowledge. *London Review of Education*, 17(1): 26–37.

Hudson, B. (2018). Powerful knowledge and epistemic quality in school mathematics. *London Review of Education*, 16(3): 384–397.

Hudson, B., Henderson, S. and Hudson, A. (2015). Developing mathematical thinking in the primary classroom: liberating students and teachers as learners of mathematics. *Journal of Curriculum Studies*, 47(3): 374–398.

Irving, W. (1828). *A History of the Life and Voyages of Christopher Columbus, Volume 1*. London: John Murray.

Jeffreys, B. (2019). Language learning: German and French drop by half in UK schools. *BBC News* (27 February). Available at: https://www.bbc.co.uk/news/education-47334374.

Jones, K. and Wiliam, D. (2022). Lethal mutations in education and how to prevent them. *Evidence Based Education* [blog] (13 October). Available at: https://evidencebased.education/lethal-mutations-in-education-and-how-to-prevent-them.

King-Hele, D. (1976). The shape of the Earth. *Science*, 192(4246): 1293–1300.

Kitson, A. (2021). How helpful is the theory of powerful knowledge for history educators? In A. Chapman (ed.), *Knowing History in Schools: Powerful Knowledge and the Powers of Knowledge*. London: UCL Press, pp. 32–50.

Lambert, D. (2011). Why subjects really matter: a personal view. Available at: https://geography.org.uk/wp-content/uploads/2023/06/David_Lambert_on_Why_subjects_really_matter__2022.pdf.

Lambert, D. (2017). GeoCapabilities. Presentation given at the Geography Teacher Educators Conference, University of Plymouth, 27–29 January.

Lambert, D. and Morgan, J. (2010). *Teaching Geography 11–18: A Conceptual Approach*. Maidenhead: Open University Press.

Lambert, D., Solem, M. and Tani, S. (2015). Achieving human potential through geography education: a capabilities approach to curriculum making in schools. *Annals of the Association of American Geographers*, 105(4): 723–735.

Lancet (2022). Editorial. *The Lancet Diabetes and Endocrinology*, 10(1): 1. Available at: https://www.thelancet.com/action/showPdf?pii=S2213-8587%2821%2900314-4.

Langer, S. K. (1957). *Problems of Art: Ten Philosophical Lectures*. New York: Scribner.

Lawes, S. (2007). Foreign languages without tears? In R. Whelan (ed.), *The Corruption of the Curriculum*. London: Civitas, pp. 86–97.

Lawes, S. (2021). Foreign languages. In A. Sehgal Cuthbert and A. Standish (eds), *What Should Schools Teach? Disciplines, Subjects and the Pursuit of Truth*, 2nd edn. London: UCL Press, pp. 122–136.

Layton, D. (1972). Science as general education. *Trends in Education*, 1072: 11–15.

Leat, D. (1998). *Thinking Through Geography*. Cambridge: Chris Kington Publishing.

Ledda, M. (2007). English as a dialect. In R. Whelan (ed.), *The Corruption of the Curriculum*. London: Civitas, pp. 11–27.

Looney, J. T. (1920). *'Shakespeare' Identified: In Edward de Vere the Seventeenth Earl of Oxford*. London: Cecil Palmer.

Lough, C. (2020). Third of teachers leaving the profession within 5 years. *TES* (25 June). Available at: https://www.tes.com/magazine/archive/third-teachers-leaving-profession-within-5-years.

Martin, M. (2023). Recruitment crisis: DfE set to miss 2023–24 targets. *TES* (23 March). Available at: https://www.tes.com/magazine/news/general/teacher-recruitment-crisis-dfe-set-flunk-2023-24-targets.

Maton, K. and Moore, R. (eds) (2010). *Social Realism, Knowledge and the Sociology of Education: Coalitions of the Mind*. London: Continuum.

Maude, A. (2016). What might powerful geographical knowledge look like? *Geography*, 101(1): 70–76.

McGovern, C. (2007). The New History boys. In R. Whelan (ed.), *The Corruption of the Curriculum*. London: Civitas, pp. 58–85.

McLean, I. (2018). What is social science? *The British Academy* [blog] (20 November). Available at: https://www.thebritishacademy.ac.uk/blog/what-social-science.

McMillan, I. (2016). Transformatio per complexitatem: the 20th century transformation of Latin teaching in the UK. *Journal of Classics Teaching*, 16(32): 25–32.

Mercer, L. (1950). Modern languages for today. *Journal of Education*, 133(4): 118–120.

Milner, C. (2020). Classroom strategies for tackling the whiteness of geography. *Teaching Geography*, 45(3): 105–107.

Mistry, J. (2009). Indigenous knowledges. In R. Kitchin and N. Thrift (eds), *International Encyclopedia of Human Geography*, Vol. 5. Oxford: Elsevier, pp. 371–376.

Mohamud, A. and Whitburn, R. (2014). Unpacking the suitcase and finding history: doing justice to the teaching of diverse histories in the classroom. *Teaching History*, 154: 40–46.

Morgan, J. and Lambert, D. (2005). *Geography: Teaching School Subjects 11–19*. Abingdon: Routledge.

Morgan, J. and Lambert, D. (2023). *Race, Racism and the Geography Curriculum*. London: Bloomsbury Academic.

Myatt, M. (2018). *The Curriculum: Gallimaufry to Coherence*. Woodbridge: John Catt Educational.

Nanji, N. (2023). Rizz named word of the year 2023 by Oxford University Press. *BBC News* (4 December). Available at: https://www.bbc.co.uk/news/entertainment-arts-67602699.

Newton, I. (1687). *Principia: The Natural Principles of Mathematical Philosophy*. London: Fleet Street.

Nussbaum, M. (1988). Nature, function and capability: Aristotle on political distribution. *Oxford Studies in Ancient Philosophy*, suppl. vol.: 145–184.

Nussbaum, M. (2000). *Women and Human Development: The Capabilities Approach*. Cambridge: Cambridge University Press.

Nussbaum, M. (2006). Education and democratic citizenship: capabilities and quality education. *Journal of Human Development*, 7(3): 385–395.

Ofcom (2022). Instagram, TikTok and YouTube teenagers' top three news sources (21 July). Available at: https://www.ofcom.org.uk/news-centre/2022/instagram,-tiktok-and-youtube-teenagers-top-three-news-sources.

Office for National Statistics (2022). UK: Religion, England and Wales: Census 2021 (29 November). Available at: https://www.ons.gov.uk/peoplepopulationandcommunity/culturalidentity/religion/bulletins/religionenglandandwales/census2021.

Pariser, E. (2011a). Beware online 'filter bubbles'. *TED* (March). Available at: https://www.ted.com/talks/eli_pariser_beware_online_filter_bubbles.

Pariser, E. (2011b). *The Filter Bubble: What the Internet Is Hiding from You*. London: Penguin.

Park, R. E. and Burgess, E. (1925). *The City*. Chicago, IL: University of Chicago Press.

Perks, D. (2007). What is science education for? In R. Whelan (ed.), *The Corruption of the Curriculum*. London: Civitas, pp. 109–139.

Powell, D. (2021). Art. In A. Sehgal Cuthbert and A. Standish (eds), *What Should Schools Teach? Disciplines, Subjects and the Pursuit of Truth*, 2nd edn. London: UCL Press, pp. 73–88.

Pruitt, S. (2023). Did Shakespeare really write his own plays? *History* (22 August). Available at: https://www.history.com/news/did-shakespeare-really-write-his-own-plays.

Puttick, S. (2020). Raising issues: taking Burgess out of the bin. *Teaching Geography*, 45(1): 6–8.

Puttick, S. and Murrey, A. (2020). Confronting the deafening silence on race in geography education in England: learning from anti-racist, decolonial and Black geographies. *Geography*, 105(3): 127–134.

Puustinen, M. and Khawaja, A. (2020). Envisaging the alternatives: from knowledge of the powerful to powerful knowledge in history classrooms. *Journal of Curriculum Studies*, 53(1): 16–31.

Qualifications and Curriculum Authority (2008). *The Curriculum: Progress and Opportunities*. London: QCA. Available at: https://dera.ioe.ac.uk/id/eprint/8784/7/1847218806_Redacted.pdf.

Ravetz, J. R. (2005). *The No-Nonsense Guide to Science*. Oxford: New Internationalist Publications.

Rawding, C. (2019). Raising issues: putting Burgess in the bin. *Teaching Geography*, 44(3): 94–96.

Rawling, E. (2000). Ideology, politics and curriculum change: reflections on school geography 2000. *Geography*, 85(3), 209–220.

Reiss, M. and White, J. (2013). *An Aims-Based Curriculum: The Significance of Human Flourishing for Schools*. London: IOE Press.

Roberts, M. (2010). UK among Europe's unhealthiest nations, report suggests. *BBC News* (14 December). Available at: https://www.bbc.co.uk/news/health-11983915.

Roberts, M. (2013). *Geography through Enquiry: Approaches to Teaching and Learning in the Secondary School.* Sheffield: Geographical Association.

Roberts, M. (2023). Powerful pedagogies for the school geography curriculum. *International Research in Geography and Environmental Education,* 32(1): 69–84.

Robinson, M. (2013). *Trivium 21c: Preparing Young People for the Future with Lessons from the Past.* Carmarthen: Independent Thinking Press.

Robinson, M. (2021). Drama. In A. S. Sehgal Cuthbert and A. Standish (eds), *What Should Schools Teach? Disciplines, Subjects and the Pursuit of Truth,* 2nd edn. London: UCL Press, pp. 89–102.

Rycroft-Smith, L. (2019). Exploring the knowledge structure of maths. *TES* (18 December). Available at: https://www.tes.com/magazine/archive/exploring-knowledge-structure-maths.

Schneider, E. (2020). *English Around the World: An Introduction,* 2nd edn. Cambridge: Cambridge University Press.

Schubert, M. M. and Broom, D. R. (2020). Exercise and diet. In H. Meiselman (ed.), *Handbook of Eating and Drinking.* Cham: Springer, pp. 787–803.

Sehgal Cuthbert, A. (2021). English literature. In A. Sehgal Cuthbert and A. Standish (eds), *What Should Schools Teach? Disciplines, Subjects and the Pursuit of Truth,* 2nd edn. London: UCL Press, pp. 54–72.

Sehgal Cuthbert, A. and Standish, A. (eds) (2021). *What Should Schools Teach? Disciplines, Subjects and the Pursuit of Truth,* 2nd edn. London: UCL Press.

Seitz-Wald, A. (2013). Actually, even the Flat Earth Society believes in climate change. *Salon* (25 June). Available at: https://www.salon.com/2013/06/25/flat_earth_society_believes_in_climate_change.

Sen, A. (1980). Equality of what? In S. McMurrin (ed.), *The Tanner Lectures on Human Values, Vol. 1.* Cambridge: Cambridge University Press, pp. 197–220. Available at: https://tannerlectures.utah.edu/_resources/documents/a-to-z/s/sen80.pdf.

Sen, A. (1985a). Well-being, agency and freedom. *Journal of Philosophy,* 82(4): 169–221.

Sen, A. (1985b). *Commodities and Capabilities.* Amsterdam: North-Holland.

Sen, A. (1987). The standard of living. In G. Hawthorn (ed.), *The Standard of Living,* Cambridge: Cambridge University Press, pp. 94–102.

Sen, A. (1999). *Development as Freedom.* Oxford: Oxford University Press.

Sen, A. (2004). Capabilities, lists and public reason: continuing the conversation. *Feminist Economics,* 10(3): 77–80.

Sharwood Smith, J. (1977). *On Teaching Classics.* London: Routledge and Kegan Paul.

Sheehan, M. (2021). *Ka Mura, Ka Muri* [Look to the past to inform the future]: disciplinary history, cultural responsiveness and Māori perspectives of the past. In A. Chapman (ed.), *Knowing History in Schools: Powerful Knowledge and the Powers of Knowledge.* London: UCL Press, pp. 202–215.

Sherrington, T. (2019). *Rosenshine's Principles in Action.* Woodbridge: John Catt Educational.

Siedentop, D. (2002). Content knowledge for physical education. *Journal of Teaching in Physical Education,* 21: 368–377.

Sky News (2016). Gove: Britons 'have had enough of experts' (3 June). Available at https://www.youtube.com/watch?v=GGgiGtJk7MA.

Smith, J. and Jackson, D. (2021). Two concepts of power: knowledge (re)production in English history education discourse. In A. Chapman (ed.), *Knowing History in Schools: Powerful Knowledge and the Powers of Knowledge.* London: UCL Press, pp. 152–176.

Smith, M. (2017). How left or right-wing are the UK's newspapers? *YouGov* (7 March). Available at: https://yougov.co.uk/topics/politics/articles-reports/2017/03/07/how-left-or-right-wing-are-uks-newspapers.

Smith, N. (2012). *Choosing How to Teach and Teaching How to Choose: Using the Three Cs to Improve Learning.* Seattle, WA: Bennett and Hastings.

Solem, M., Lambert, D. and Tani, S. (2013). GeoCapabilities: toward an international framework for researching the purposes and values of geography education. *Review of International Geographical Education,* 3(3): 214–229. Available at: https://rigeo.org/menu-script/index.php/rigeo/article/view/204/190.

Solvason, C. (2010). Elitism, inclusion and the specialist school. In G. Elliott, C. Fourali and S. Issler (eds), *Education and Social Change: Connecting Local and Global Perspectives*. London: Continuum, pp. 122–135.

SSCE Cymru (n.d.). Service families learning Welsh. Available at: https://www.sscecymru.co.uk/servicefamilies/learningwelsh/default.htm.

Standish, A. (2007). Geography used to be about maps. In R. Whelan (ed.), *The Corruption of the Curriculum*. London: Civitas, pp. 28–57.

Stewart, F. (2001). Book review: *Women and Human Development: The Capabilities Approach* by Martha C. Nussbaum. *Journal of International Development*, 13(8): 1191–1192.

Sturdy, G. (2021). Physics. In A. Sehgal Cuthbert and A. Standish (eds), *What Should Schools Teach? Disciplines, Subjects and the Pursuit of Truth*, 2nd edn. London: UCL Press, pp. 218–233.

Svendsen, A. M. and Svendsen, J. T. (2016). Teacher or coach? How logics from the field of sports contribute to the construction of knowledge in PETE pedagogical discourse through educational texts. *Sport, Education and Society*, 21(5): 796–810.

Tanaka, S. (2011). The notion of embodied knowledge. In P. Stenner, J. Cromby, J. Motzaku, J. Yen and Y. Haosheng (eds), *Theoretical Psychology: Global Transformations and Challenges*. Ontario: Captus Press, pp. 149–157.

Terzi, L. (2005). *Equality, Capability and Justice in Education: Towards a Principled Framework for a Just Distribution of Educational Resources to Disabled Learners*. Paper prepared for the fifth International Conference on the Capability Approach: Knowledge and Public Action. Paris, 11–14 September. Available at: https://www.researchgate.net/profile/Lorella_Terzi/publication/253934371_Equality_Capability_and_Justice_in_Education_Towards_a_Principled_Framework_for_a_Just_Distribution_of_Educational_Resources_to_Disabled_Learners/links/0deec5304cc288b1cd000000.pdf.

Tett, G. (2010). The story of the Brics. *Financial Times* (15 January). Available at: https://www.ft.com/content/112ca932-00ab-11df-ae8d-00144feabdc0.

Tinning, R. (2002). Engaging Siedentopian perspectives on content knowledge for physical education. *Journal of Teaching in Physical Education*, 21: 378–391.

Tinning, R. (2015). Commentary on research into learning in physical education: towards a mature field of knowledge. *Sport, Education and Society*, 20(5): 676–690.

Tirtha, B. K. (1965). *Vedic Mathematics*. Delhi: Motilal Banarsidass.

Toyne, S. (2021). Music. In A. Sehgal Cuthbert and A. Standish (eds), *What Should Schools Teach? Disciplines, Subjects and the Pursuit of Truth*, 2nd edn. London: UCL Press, pp. 103–121.

Tubb, C. (2003). Moral education. In J. Beck and M. Earl (eds), *Key Issues in Secondary Education*. London: Continuum, pp. 147–157.

Turner, C. and Somerville, E. (2020). Shakespeare, Blake and Woolf are on the curriculum due to 'racial bias', university says. *The Telegraph* (31 January).

Usborne, E., Peck, J., Smith, D. L. and Taylor, D. M. (2011). Learning through an Aboriginal language: the impact on students' English and Aboriginal language skills. *Canadian Journal of Education/Revue canadienne de l'éducation*, 34(4): 200–215.

Vasagar, J. and Herbert, T. (2012). School playing fields: 21 sell-offs have been approved by coalition. *The Guardian* (6 August). Available at: https://www.theguardian.com/education/2012/aug/06/school-playing-field-sale-gove.

Venville, G., Rennie, L. and Wallace, J. (2012). Curriculum integration: challenging the assumption of school science as a powerful knowledge. In B. Fraser, K. Tobin and C. McRobbie (eds), *Second International Handbook of Science Education*. Dordrecht: Springer, pp. 737–749.

Walker, M. (2006). *Higher Education Pedagogies: A Capabilities Approach*. Maidenhead: Society for Research into Higher Education and Open University Press.

Walker, M. and Unterhalter, E. (eds) (2007). *Amartya Sen's Capability Approach and Social Justice in Education*. London: Palgrave Macmillan.

Walshe, N. and Perry, J. (2022). Transformative geography education: developing eco-capabilities for a flourishing and sustainable future. *Teaching Geography*, 47(3): 94–97.

Ward, H. (2018). Curriculum must cover more than 'dead, white men' – Bousted. *TES* (7 June). Available at: https://www.tes.com/magazine/archive/curriculum-must-cover-more-dead-white-men-bousted.

Weale, S. (2022). Teachers encouraged to use Taylor Swift lyrics to make Latin accessible. *The Guardian* (7 April). Available at: https://www.theguardian.com/education/2022/apr/07/teachers-encouraged-to-use-taylor-swift-lyrics-to-make-latin-accessible.

Whelan, R. (ed.) (2007). *The Corruption of the Curriculum*. London: Civitas.

White, J. (2018). The weakness of 'powerful knowledge'. *London Review of Education*, 16(2): 325–335.

White, J. (2019). The end of powerful knowledge? *London Review of Education*, 17(3): 429–438.

Whitesides, J. (2020). Trump's handling of coronavirus pandemic hits record low approval: Reuters/Ipsos poll. *Reuters* (8 October). Available at: https://www.reuters.com/article/us-usa-election-trump-coronavirus-idUSKBN26T3OF.

Wilby, P. (2018). The counterculture class warrior who turned to Gove. *The Guardian* (9 October). Available at: https://www.theguardian.com/education/2018/oct/09/counterculture-class-warrior-turned-to-gove.

Willingham, D. (2021). *Why Don't Students Like School? A Cognitive Scientist Answers Questions About How the Mind Works and What It Means for the Classroom*, 2nd edn. San Fransisco, CA: Jossey-Bass.

Wimsatt, W. K., Jr. and Beardsley, M. C. (1946). The intentional fallacy. *The Sewanee Review*, 54(3): 468–488.

Wintersgill, B. (ed.) (2017). *Big Ideas for Religious Education*. Exeter: University of Exeter.

Wolfe, S. (n.d.). Iconic artworks: Banksy's shredded painting – art or prank? *Artland Magazine*. Available at: https://magazine.artland.com/banksy-shredded-painting.

Women in Sport (2024). More girls are playing football but a significant team sport gender gap remains [press release] (2 February). Available at: https://womeninsport.org/news/more-girls-are-playing-football-but-a-significant-team-sport-gender-gap-remains.

Wootton, D. (2015). *The Invention of Science: A New History of the Scientific Revolution*. London: Penguin.

Wright, D. and Taverner, S. (2009). *Thinking Through Mathematics*. Cambridge: Chris Kington Publishing.

Yates, L. and Millar, V. (2016). 'Powerful knowledge' curriculum theories and the case of physics. *Curriculum Journal*, 27(3): 298–312.

Young, M. (1971). *Knowledge and Control: New Directions for the Sociology of Education*. London: Collier-Macmillan.

Young, M. (2008). *Bringing Knowledge Back In: From Social Constructivism to Social Realism in the Sociology of Education*. Abingdon: Routledge.

Young, M. and Lambert, D. (2014). *Knowledge and the Future School: Curriculum and Social Justice*. London: Bloomsbury.

Young, M. and Muller, J. (2010). Three educational scenarios for the future: lessons from the sociology of knowledge. *European Journal of Education*, 45(1): 11–27.